GOING
DEEPER

GOING DEEPER

TED ROBERTS & PAM VREDEVELT

Foursquare Media

Scripture quotations marked AMP are from the Amplified Bible. Old Testament copyright © 1965, 1987 by the Zondervan Corporation. The Amplified New Testament copyright © 1954, 1958, 1987 by the Lockman Foundation. Used by permission.

Scripture quotations marked CEV are from the Contemporary English Version, copyright © 1995 by the American Bible Society. Used by permission.

Scripture quotations marked GWT are from God's Word. Copyright © 1995 by God's Word to the Nations. All rights reserved. Used by permission.

Hebrew word definitions are from *New International Dictionary of Old Testament Theology and Exegesis*, edited by Willem A. Van Gemeran. Grand Rapids, MI: Zondervan, 1997.

Cover design by Terry Clifton

Library of Congress Control Number: 2006935145
International Standard Book Number-10: 1-59979-081-5
International Standard Book Number-13: 978-1-59979-081-7

07 08 09 10 — 9 8 7 6 5 4 3 2
Printed in the United States of America

CONTENTS

FOREWORD

*T*AKING THIS BOOK in hand may well determine your ability to take your future in hand—especially as things are shaping up in our world as *Going Deeper* comes off the presses. It is not a time in which any one of us can afford living in "the shallows."

Our present moment is laden with weighty world events that are too seldom met realistically. "The shallows" are those "sound bite" analyses and "quick fix" answers that are the stock in trade of a media-fixated society. So in saying, this book can shape your future with the right stuff, I am not being melodramatic. To the contrary, I couldn't be more passionate about anything than I am about the implications for you as you begin your study of what the following pages have to offer.

Yes, it is a study—but, no, it isn't boring—or hard to grasp. That is because Ted Roberts's writing has a way of being paced by his background as a jet fighter pilot: it never lags, drags, or sags. In writing these pages he has teamed with Pam Vredeveldt, and you will be moved forward with a momentum fueled by their passion and experience at helping people like you start and keep growing at life's most significant dimension—our relationship with God.

Going Deeper is a reflection of the kind of leadership Ted has given as pastor of one of Oregon's largest churches—the congregation at Easthill, in Gresham, a part of the Portland metroplex. That is where these insights were first presented before he and Pam fashioned this package for widespread use—where crowds come because of more than mere excitement. They come because they have found a place where depth hasn't been traded for appeal.

Let me explain.

There is a false supposition today that to be contemporary, spiritual things need to be diluted—as though our deepest hunger can be satisfied with a swig of God, rather than drinking deeply of His life and love. But the truth is, it is an empty exchange to sacrifice depth for appeal, and it is proven on these pages.

Depth and appeal not only belong together—the majority of thoughtful people will not settle for "shallow" anyway!

Going Deeper is about opening to what God's Word teaches, and what Jesus Christ says about the Holy Spirit—the third Person of what theologians call "the Trinity." That term is simply a pointer, hinting at the grandeur and wonder of the marvel and mystery inherent in God's greatness—a vastness in His being, His love, and His power that exceeds explanation. Still, this much is certain: God has made enough of Himself clear that when we are ready to take the plunge into really knowing Him, we will never be disappointed.

The river of God's love, goodness, and miraculous ways is one of increasing depth and power, and He invites us to "come"—to first, drink at the fountain of His saving goodness, then swim in the river of His power. (Read Ezekiel 47:1–9!)

So move ahead: open the following pages, and join me and the multitudes today who are saying, "I've had it with 'the shallows!'"

In the adventure of following Jesus Christ,

—JACK W. HAYFORD
PRESIDENT, INTERNATIONAL FOURSQUARE CHURCHES
CHANCELLOR, THE KING'S COLLEGE AND SEMINARY
FOUNDING PASTOR, THE CHURCH ON THE WAY
SEPTEMBER, 2006
LOS ANGELES, CALIFORNIA

INTRODUCTION
THE FIRE OF HIS LOVE

Ted Roberts

*T*IGHTLY STRAPPED INTO my high performance fighter aircraft, I ducked and dodged my way through a world of infinite darkness. Just seconds before, I watched a plane off my left wing explode into a searing fireball and soar into oblivion. A surface to air missile had hit its target. Shaken by the pyrotechnic explosion and the possible demise of my fellow pilot, I repeated to myself for the thousandth time that we were on a mission, and we would accomplish that mission.

It was 1970, and the Vietnam War had reached a new level of insanity. News from home depicted our beloved nation being ripped apart at the seams by polarized opinions. Could the war be won the way it was being fought? Should we be in the war at all?

Somewhere along the way, my childhood dream of flying a fighter aircraft had morphed into a nightmare. Frankly, I was thankful just to be alive. Many of the men fighting alongside me to stop the spread of Communism hadn't made it. For the rest of us, each day—each hour—of life was a gift of grace.

Approaching the airfield I dropped my landing gear and flaps. Suddenly ground fire flew by my aircraft from all directions. Bright tracers arched past the cockpit. Small arms fired and launched from one of the villages I was risking my life to defend. Maneuvering the plane down onto the landing strip, I screamed, "This is nuts!"

Welcome to the sheer lunacy of guerilla war. There are no front lines. You can daily defeat the enemy on the battlefield and still lose the war.

But I was losing more than comrades. I was losing my sanity. God knew. He saw my madness. He was well aware of the nightmares that haunted the hallways of my mind late into the night. Hellish scenes replayed over and over again in vivid Technicolor. A fifth of Jack Daniels couldn't stop the tormenting intrusions.

But there was a positive side to all of this. My bride back home was praying. Now you need to know something about Diane. When she prays, God moves. On this particular evening, He answered the cry of her heart by grabbing hold of me through her love letter.

It was waiting for me at my barracks. Recognizing Diane's handwriting on the envelope, I eagerly slipped my pocketknife through the seal. The fragrance of her favorite perfume filled the air, transporting me home, even if only for a moment.

Her words breathed fresh hope into the heart of this weary Marine. I couldn't deny the purity of her devotion to me. She had loved me when I was unlovable. She'd stuck with me when I was absorbed in personal pursuits and couldn't see beyond the end of my nose.

Diane also loved Jesus, and made no apologies telling me so. Her letter got straight to the point: "Ted, Jesus loves you. He died on the cross for your sins and for mine. He wants both of us to experience forgiveness and to spend eternity together."

My wife had spoken of her love for Christ before, but this time it was different. This time she scored a direct hit. Her words slipped through all of my elaborate defenses and penetrated the core of my soul. Right there, in the middle of a rocket attack, I knelt in the bunker I had run to for safety.

I wasn't kneeling in fear. I was used to the war zone, and well accustomed to wailing sirens and the "thump-thump" of 122-millimeter rockets pulverizing the ground. No, I wasn't kneeling in fear. I was kneeling in desperation. I knew I was losing my mind, and needed God. He got an uncensored earful that night:

> Well, God, I have always believed in You. I'll admit I've ignored You. But I have always known You were there. Now I don't understand who the _____ _____ this Jesus Christ is, but sign me up!

It was a turning point for me. It was the night I began the incredible adventure of opening my life to the influence of a supernatural God.

The Encounter

The beginning of this spiritual journey was a bit rocky. The few Christians I brushed shoulders with seemed mostly concerned about appearances, rules, and regulations. They talked church language, but their walk didn't match their talk. To be honest, that brand of Christianity had no appeal for me at all.

After my tour in Vietnam, I returned stateside, continuing my tour of duty as a Marine flight instructor in Kingsville, Texas. Shortly thereafter I began looking for a place of worship to help me grow in my newfound faith.

The search was mostly disappointing. The church atmosphere seemed stiff. The religious jargon was confusing. The sermons seemed irrelevant and out of touch with things that were on my mind. Yet despite these discouragements, a gnawing hunger to know God persisted, driving me to look further.

While stationed in Texas, Diane asked if we could visit a radical ministry that helped street kids and drug addicts. I heard the word "radical" and thought, *Well, why not? It has to be better than church.* Beneath all that bravado, however, my heart was looking for an answer to a daily battle that was pulling me down. It was alcoholism, and it had me in its grip. I was desperate for solutions. The wicked nightmares and flashbacks I brought home from Vietnam were only getting worse. And so was the drinking.

I was ill prepared, however, for what I encountered that night as we walked into the storefront coffeehouse where the meeting was being held. I couldn't believe my eyes. I had never seen so many weird-looking, be-bopping hippies in all my days. A career in the Marine Corps obviously reduces the number of men you meet with hair hanging down to their knees. This place was loaded with them! *Oh, great!* I thought. *I've gone from one insane asylum to another.*

In the commotion of the crowd I lost sight of Diane. Ten minutes later I found someone who looked fairly coherent and asked him if he knew where my wife had gone.

"Dude, she's in the back praying with some of the brothers," he gushed, with a ridiculous expression on his face. I strode quickly to the back and encountered a scene straight out of Looney Tunes. Everyone was talking to God out loud, and Diane was in the middle of this madness, smiling from ear to ear. *What in the world was this?*

Turning to the group leader I blurted out, "What the heck is going on?"

Calm and cool, he responded, "Your wife is asking God to fill her with His Holy Spirit." I started to reach through the noisy crowd to pull her out of there, but something stopped me. I didn't fully understand what was happening, but somehow I sensed the presence of God in the mix.

"Would you like the Spirit of God to fill you, too?" the leader asked me.

The words that flew from my mouth surprised me, "Sure. How do you do that?"

"Just ask Him," he replied. "Ask God to fill you with His Holy Spirit."

I paused, stared him straight in the eye, and said, "Jesus, fill my life with the Holy Spirit. Now, I'm taking my wife out of here before I punch somebody's lights out!"

The man rapidly stepped backwards, eyes as big as quarters. "No problem!" he said. "Fine. Go right ahead!"

On the way home that night, I told Diane that we were never going back to that crazy place again. God only knows what I might do the next time. I envisioned myself decking a few of those long hairs. Undaunted by anything I said, Diane sat next to me, a sparkling smile lighting up her whole countenance.

The Coming of Fire

The next day was business as usual; or so I thought. I stepped out into the withering heat of a Texas summer day. On top of the humidity, the air was shot through with the mingled smells of jet fuel, burning asphalt, and human sweat. It was the smell of my work-a-day world, and as familiar to me as an old friend.

My job was introducing fledgling pilots to the intricacies of bombing. It had its challenges. Maneuvering three student pilots into the air so that they arrived at the practice range within a ten-minute window can only be compared to herding a group of wild cats!

Exploding out of the maintenance shack, I strode to the flight line. I was ticked. I'd just discovered that the aircraft assigned to me that day had numerous problems. But the clock was ticking, and time was tight. Since it was late in the day, most of the better planes were already gone. I got the runt of the litter. Barreling down the flight line, I noticed the plane captain coming toward me. He was a young sailor who looked to me like a disheveled mess—irritating my Marine Corps spit and polish. Oblivious to what he was supposed to do, he just stood there in a daze, overwhelmed by the roar of the jet engines and everything happening around him.

The plane wasn't even close to being ready for inspection, let alone takeoff. Hydraulic fluid was smeared down the side of one of the landing gears, access panels were hanging open, and the last thing I wanted to deal with was a semi-conscious sailor in grungy overalls.

Eventually I managed to patch up the plane so that it was in stable flying condition. Climbing into the cockpit, I waited for the plane captain to assist me with the gymnastics required in strapping on a high performance fighter aircraft. He was nowhere in sight! That was the final straw! I promised myself that I would tear into this guy after we returned.

Prepared to start the engine, I felt a hint of relief when the captain appeared to the left of the aircraft. Maybe we'd take off on time, after all. The startup procedure progressed smoothly. I glanced out of the cockpit once again, signaling to the sailor that I was going to check the proper functioning of the flight controls.

I "swept the cockpit" as we called it, moving the control stick in a counter clockwise circle. The plane captain ever-so-carefully observed the control surfaces to see if everything was working correctly. Patience was never my long suit. I slammed the stick around the cockpit, irritated over being behind schedule.

Flashing me a huge smile, the young man gave me thumbs up, and at that very instant, something supernatural happened. I don't know how else to explain it. Catching me completely off guard, an overwhelming sense of love suddenly erupted from inside me and overflowed towards this young man. Anger disappeared. Irritation vanished. God's presence swept across me like a cleansing spring shower. *What in the world?* It stunned me. Nothing like this had ever happened to me before. I can't even describe the compassion I felt for the young sailor—someone I'd never met before. It was as if I could see into his soul. I understood his fears and his desire to please. I saw how harsh and intimidating I had been. And I knew very well the love I felt towards him in that moment was not my own.

All I could do was weep. Tears coursed down my face. *Oh great*, I thought. *Here's the battle-seasoned Marine suddenly crying like a baby in front of a sailor!* Quickly turning my face away, I lowered the visor on my helmet to hide the emotion. *I'm losing it*, I said to myself. *This must be some sort of delayed stress syndrome.*

At that point, I didn't have a clue. It hadn't even occurred to me that what was happening had any connection to my prayer the night before and that the Holy Spirit was engulfing me in the radiant warmth of God's fierce love. It was as if the experience had come out of another dimension. And it had. This was the realm of the Spirit, an unknown territory for me.

God's outrageous love roared like a prairie fire through my calloused soul. I was in His furnace of transformation. It scared me. It filled me with wonder. It made me want to laugh and cry at the same time. The Holy Spirit was purging impurities within me and stoking a furious passion for the things of God. My soul blazed with His presence. His fire cleansed. His fire healed.

Fire Leaves Its Mark

Do you ever remember sitting in front of a campfire as a kid, trying to figure out fire? I mean, what is it? It has no fixed shape or substance. You can't grasp it. You can't touch it without being affected, changed.

In the Bible, God frequently represents Himself as fire—from the pillar of fire that led God's people through the wilderness, to the leaping tongues of fire that danced atop the disciple's heads on the day of Pentecost. The risen Christ kindled a fire on the beach to prepare breakfast for Simon Peter, who had denied Him. And in the blinding majesty of His second coming, the Son of God will thunder back into human history astride a white horse—His eyes a flame of fire.

Make no mistake; fire always leaves its mark. Ever since my encounter with God in that cockpit, I have passionately hungered to know Him better, to more fully comprehend His ways, and to have a closer relationship with Him.

Through the years I became acquainted with great men and women of faith who challenged me to pursue the depths of God. Because of my scientific background in mathematics and astrophysics, I was naturally drawn to Blaise Pascal. One of the most brilliant minds of his era, Pascal established the principles of hydrodynamics, the theory of probability, and the foundations of differential and integral calculus. When Pascal died, loved ones happened across the following memo sewn into the lining of his coat:

> In the year of Grace 1654,
> From about half past ten in the evening until about
> half past twelve,
> FIRE
> God of Abraham, God of Isaac, God of Jacob,
> Not of the philosophers and scholars.
> Certitude, Certitude. Feeling. Joy. Peace.
> God of Jesus Christ...
> JESUS CHRIST
>
> I have separated myself from Him: I have fled from
> Him, denied Him, crucified Him.
> Let me never be separated from Him.
> Renunciation, total and sweet.
> Eternally in joy for a day's training on earth.
> Amen.[1]

On an evening in 1654 when the great mathematician was reading Scripture, God revealed Himself to him. Pascal encountered the risen Christ while reading the seventeenth chapter of John's Gospel, which records Christ's priestly prayer for all of us.

God's love letters in Pascal's hands were confirmed by the manifest presence of Jesus Christ.

Consumed by God's fiery love, Pascal bowed in total submission to Jesus Christ. The penitent scholar was instantly aware of the absolute futility of living for oneself. All his intellectual pursuits and scholarly renown paled in comparison to the consuming love of God. During times of adversity, I can only imagine how often he slipped his hand over his jacket and pressed those words to his heart.

Pascal's writings describe what I had experienced in the cockpit that day. Ever since that day I have had an insatiable passion for a closer, deeper relationship with God. I have longed to know God the Father and Jesus, God's Son. I have sought to understand the person of the Holy Spirit, whose ongoing and ultimate desire is to bring honor to Christ. I have grappled to find words that adequately explain the mystery of experiencing God's Spirit living and moving within me, and His church. I have repeatedly asked God for wisdom about how to help others who hunger for more of God in their lives, too.

My co-author, Pam Vredevelt, shares similar passions. Pam loves God and has committed her life to helping people come to know Him in deeply personal ways. She and her husband, John, who is one of my assistant pastors, have faithfully served the people at East Hill Church for over thirty years. I've asked Pam to co-write this book with me because of her devotion to God, her clinical insight, and her ability to communicate biblical truths in relevant terms for this generation. We have contributed equally to the content and shaping of this book.

Together, we want to take you on a treasure hunt through God's love letters, with special focus on the Book of Ephesians. We are asking the person of the Holy Spirit to lead you into experiential encounters with God as He teaches you how to access the vast spiritual wealth that is yours in Christ Jesus.

Cutting Through the Confusion

There is so much confusion today about the Holy Spirit. Some shy away from Him for fear of moving into error. They see anything mystical as an open door to doctrinal inaccuracy. They guard against seeking experiences with God, because history has shown that many have given more authority to their experiences than to the Word of God. Worse yet, some have based their beliefs on experiences that don't align with Scripture, and have been grossly deceived.

While this has been the case, there are numerous accounts in the Bible, and throughout history, where Christian men and women have had experiential encounters with the Spirit of God that radically changed their lives. These divine encounters ushered them into deeper intimacy with God, led them to make drastic life changes that glorified Christ, and paved the way for exponential increases in their effectiveness for the kingdom of God.

This is what we, as the writers of this book, personally cry out for. We hunger to be so consumed by the Person of the Holy Spirit that we are compelled to seek an ever-deepening, experiential knowledge of the fullness of God; a fullness which transforms us from the inside out and spills over onto others in eternally significant ways.

At the same time, we trust in and depend upon the Spirit of truth to guard us from error and deception in our quest to go deeper with Him.

While some shy away from studies on the Holy Spirit. Others over-focus on Him. Their emphasis seems to start and stop with the gifts of the Holy Spirit. Not much is said about God the Father, or about Jesus Christ. This is a serious problem because the Lord Jesus clearly taught that the Holy Spirit would not glorify Himself, but the Son.

Jesus said:

When He, the Spirit of truth, has come, He will guide you into all truth; for He will not speak on His own authority, but whatever He hears He will speak; and He will tell you things to come. He will glorify Me, for He will take of what is Mine and declare it to you. All things that the Father has are Mine. Therefore I said that He will take of Mine and declare it to you.

—JOHN 16:13–15, NKJV

What is it that Jesus wants the Spirit to take from Him and give to us? What might Jesus be saying right now to the Holy Spirit, to declare to us? What spiritual blessings have we inherited in Christ? What riches await our discovery in the Spirit realm? What truths might the Holy Spirit want to lead us into as we seek a deeper relationship with God?

In the pages that follow, we hope you will listen for answers to these questions as you study the Bible with us. It is our prayer that the person of the Holy Spirit, who lives within you, will lead you into dynamic encounters with the living God. While you read, meditate, pray, and interact with others in your small group. We hope you will fall more deeply in love with God as the Holy Spirit opens your understanding to the depths of His magnificent love for you.

This book is not written for those who are casual about their faith. It is intended for those who, in spite of being turned off by either rigid legalism or wild emotionalism in church, hunger for more of God. It is written for those who have invited Jesus Christ to be their Savior and Lord, and want to become more experientially aware of God's abiding presence in their daily life.

Finally, it is written for those who want to invigorate their faith and grow in their understanding of how God's Spirit lives in and transforms His people. From the very beginning, we had in mind readers who long for fresh perspective on what it means to live the Spirit-filled life and yearn for more depth in their relationship with God.

+ Do you ever suffer deep and abiding weariness that tempts you to throw in the towel in the midst of a long fight?

+ Are exhaustion and spiritual fatigue eroding your sense of hope?

+ Do you ever feel like parts of your life are in a vise, confined by immoveable clamps of constraint?

+ Does your soul hunger for freedom?

+ Do you ever feel powerless to cope with the endless string of stubborn problems life dishes up?

+ Are you eager to know God better?

+ Do you long for more intimate communion with God, and desire to fine-tune your ability to hear and respond to His voice in the midst of the daily grind?

If so, come on! Let's go deeper.

Chapter 1

The One Who Seals

Ted Roberts

J ACQUES COUSTEAU HAD a dream of penetrating the ocean depths, and it nearly cost him his life. In the 1930s he designed an underwater breathing device that filtered out carbon dioxide from exhaled oxygen. On his first ocean test-dive with the device he descended below forty-five feet and suddenly found himself in grave peril.

"My lips began to tremble uncontrollably," he wrote, "and my spine bent backwards like a bow."[1] Somehow he managed to tear off his weight belt before losing consciousness and floating to the surface. His attentive crew hauled him aboard immediately and revived him, but not without cost. Excruciating pain racked his body for weeks following this nearly fatal dive.

His dream to go deeper eclipsed the disappointment of this failed pursuit. In 1943, Cousteau invented another device, the Aqua-Lung, which fed divers compressed air on demand whenever they naturally inhaled. It also automatically matched the air pressure with the surrounding water pressure to protect a diver's lungs from being damaged.

Cousteau tested the device off the coast of France doing

underwater somersaults and barrel rolls as he descended deeper and deeper. In characteristic Cousteau fashion, he exulted, "From this day forward mankind will swim across miles of country no man has ever known…At night I have often had visions of flying by extending my arms as wings…today I flew without wings."[2]

Cousteau filmed over one hundred fifty documentaries and wrote dozens of books about his underwater adventures. Topped with his trademark red cap and behind the wheel of his high tech research vessel, the *Calypso*, Cousteau led expeditions from Alaska to the Aegean; from the frigid waters of the Atlantic to the steamy Amazon.

I have a keen appreciation for all Jacques Cousteau contributed to the sciences and the study of marine life. Thanks to his lifelong quest, I have enjoyed the thrill of scuba diving in the Caribbean and the chilly waters of the Pacific Northwest and Canada. There is nothing I would rather do for fun and refreshment than scuba dive.

But as much as I enjoy exploring the depths of the sea, it doesn't even come close to the delight and fulfillment I've discovered exploring the depths of God.

Untapped Resources

There is an insatiable hunger within me to more fully know and experience God during the years I have left in this world. I believe you share a similar passion, or you wouldn't be reading a book about going deeper in your relationship with God. I sense a similar yearning in the apostle Paul's writings, particularly in his letter to those he had served and loved in the port city of Ephesus.

Paul wrote the Ephesian letter while imprisoned in Rome, awaiting trial. Would this imprisonment end in his execution? It was possible, but he didn't know. Under the inspiration of the

Holy Spirit, Paul wasted no time and jumped into the critical truths he wanted his friends to remember:

> Praise the God and Father of our Lord Jesus Christ! Through Christ, God has blessed us with every spiritual blessing that heaven has to offer.
> —EPHESIANS 1:3, GWT

Paul immediately points to our incredible wealth in Christ. Friend, it would blow your mind if you could see an accurate picture of all that God made available to you in the spirit realm when you decided to follow Jesus. You are loaded with spiritual affluence.

It may be that you aren't aware of these spiritual blessings. Perhaps no one has alerted you to these riches. If that's the case, you have a storehouse of untapped spiritual resources awaiting you.

Get ready! God intends to take you on the adventure of your life into the high places of blessing in Him. As you make your way through this book, you are going to learn what it means to participate in the celebration of His lavish gift giving.

You Bear Heaven's Seal

The door to heaven's resources is wide open. Those who bear God's seal have the authority to enter in. Paul says:

> You heard and believed the message of truth, the Good News that He [Jesus] has saved you. In him you were *sealed with the Holy Spirit* whom he promised.
> —EPHESIANS 1:13, GWT, EMPHASIS ADDED

When you trusted Christ as your Savior, the Holy Spirit came to live within your heart. The deposit of God's Spirit in your innermost being guarantees your full inheritance of God's spiritual blessings. The seal of the Holy Spirit is like an engagement ring from God—a pledge signifying His uncompromising commitment to love you and share His wealth with you.

> This signet [or ring] from God is the first installment on what's coming, a reminder that we'll get everything God has planned for us, a praising and glorious life.
>
> —Ephesians 1:14, The Message

When Diane and I were married, we exchanged wedding rings with each other. Our rings of gold symbolized our pure and never-ending union. When we entered into the covenant of marriage, we vowed to love and cherish one another until our time on earth was complete. All that is mine is Diane's. All that is Diane's is mine. We are one in spirit.

From the moment you said yes to Christ, the Spirit of God joined with your spirit and came to live inside you. Your spirit was reborn. The Holy Spirit is with you to personally lead you and teach you how to function in the spirit realm so that you can honor Christ. Your union with the Holy Spirit gives you the privilege and authority to receive all that heaven has to offer.

In fact, *God has blessings for you that can only be accessed in the Spirit.*

> He brings gifts into our lives, much the same way the fruit appears in an orchard—things like affection for others, exuberance about life, serenity. We develop a willingness to stick with things, a sense of compassion in the heart, and a conviction that a basic holiness permeates things and people. We find ourselves involved in loyal commitments, not needing to force our way in life, able to marshal and direct our energies wisely.
>
> —Galatians 5:22–23, The Message

The Holy Spirit gives you the ability to hear the Father's voice. He enables you to sense God nudging you in certain directions. He brings particular things to your mind and prompts you to pray. He initiates dreams, and births vision in you according to the overall purpose of the Father's will. He sensitizes and prepares you for transitions just over the horizon. He grants insights that become like bright searchlights as you navigate the dark nights of your soul.

God's indwelling Spirit engineers and energizes deep, long-lasting change, transforming you to become more like Christ. He shows you how to win battles against the powers of hell that seek to kill, rob, and destroy you and your loved ones. He raises your awareness of needs the Father wants to meet in you and through you. His power touches the broken and sick in ways that bring supernatural results.

These spiritual blessings aren't just for the Mother Teresas or Billy Grahams of this world. They are for all who have said yes to Jesus and belong to Him.

Perhaps you find yourself responding, "I don't know about all of this. I've been a Christian for years, and I've never seen things in the spirit realm. I've never heard God's voice in my ears, saying, 'Go this way, or that way.' I've never witnessed a miracle. In fact, some of the people I've met who make those kinds of claims are weird—and maybe just a few bricks short of a full load."

I understand. I've encountered those folks, too, and probably shy away from them the same way you would. Unfortunately, there have always been perversions, counterfeits, and distortions of the real thing. But a counterfeit twenty-dollar bill doesn't cancel the value of an authentic twenty-dollar bill. Let's not stand back from God's rich, generous gifts simply because someone else may be confused or misrepresent Him. Let's go deeper in our quest for God and learn to discern that which is authentically His. Let's settle for nothing less than our full spiritual inheritance.

Jesus Was Sealed by the Spirit

Jesus was the first to be sealed by the Spirit after being baptized in the chilly waters of the Jordan River: "Jesus came from Nazareth in Galilee and was baptized by John in the Jordan. As Jesus was coming up out of the water, he saw heaven being torn open and the Spirit descending on him like a dove. And a voice came from heaven: 'You are my Son, whom I love; with you I am well pleased'" (Mark 1:9–11).

Jesus later referred to this moment in his life as the time when God set his seal upon Him (John 6:27).

In quick succession, three things happened to Jesus during this spiritual experience. The heavens opened. The Spirit descended. And the Father spoke.

Jesus saw heaven being torn open. The sky didn't part in a physical sense, like the waters of the Red Sea. The clouds didn't roll back like a scroll. It was a tearing open of the spiritual realm. The invisible realities of the spirit became perceptible. The spiritual realm became a functional, perceived arena of impending activity.[3]

The invisible realm of the spirit is very different than the material world we live in—that which we can see, taste, touch, hear, or smell with our natural senses. The realm of the spirit is naturally supernatural. The realm of the spirit is eternal. How "real" is it? It is infinitely more real and lasting than our temporary, material world. The domain of the spirit is the superior reality.

You and I are first and foremost spirit beings. Our spirit lives in our body, which operates in the natural realm. But the spirit realm is every bit as real and active as the natural realm. God, who is Spirit, is committed to teaching us how to perceive and function in His realm—the realm of the Spirit (2 Cor. 3:17).

If you have said yes to Christ, His Spirit lives within you, and He will continually prompt you towards an ever-deepening relationship with God. You are safe with the Holy Spirit. He will never push you or force you to do anything out of character with Christ. The more you grow in your relationship with God, the more the supernatural will seem natural. The more you seek God, the more He will draw your attention to the unseen rather than to the seen (Col. 3:2). He will urge you to turn your attention away from the temporal into the eternal (2 Cor. 4:18). He will teach you that His domain, the realm of the invisible, is neither weird nor scary.

When the Holy Spirit descended on Jesus, the invisible realm became visible. Notice the story doesn't say that the *bystanders* saw the heavens open up. It doesn't say that those watching John baptize Jesus heard the voice from heaven. There is no evidence in any accounts of this incident that the people standing on the riverbank saw or heard anything unusual that day.

There are many times in the Bible when God spoke to groups of people. But this time, He spoke only to His Son. What happened that day was all for Jesus' benefit.

As the Spirit placed His seal upon the Son, Jesus heard the familiar and affirming voice of His Father, saying: "You are my Son, whom I love; with you I am well pleased" (Mark 1:11).

God the Father knew what Jesus, the God-man, needed. He knew that many other voices would bombard His Son. Voices of disapproval, shame, and ridicule. Voices that sneered, mocked, lied, betrayed, and questioned His identity and mission. Voices that tantalized and tempted. For instance, the next voice Jesus heard following this event was Satan's, when he taunted Him in the wilderness, "If you are the Son of God" (Matt. 4:3).

Religious voices attacked Him for spending time in the company of tax collectors, prostitutes, and other condemned misfits of society. Common folk enthusiastically cheered, "Show us a miracle! Then we'll believe You." Others pleaded in desperation, "Let us make You our king!" The final jeers Jesus heard while suffering on the cross were, "Come down from the cross, if you are the Son of God" (Matt. 27:22).

All His life Jesus was surrounded by voices vying for His attention. Teach me. Feed me. Help me. Heal me. Deliver me. Give me. Yet, He never lost heart, and He was never confused about who He was or where He was headed. Remember, Jesus was God, but deliberately laid aside His divine power and prerogatives to live among us, experiencing every emotion and temptation you and I experience (Phil. 2:5–8).

How He was able to carry on? What gave Him the ability to press through the chronic chaos and fierce opposition with such world-defying assurance? One answer comes to mind. He had continual interaction with His Father by the power of the Spirit.

Now permit me to ask an obvious question or two: If *Jesus* needed the power of the Holy Spirit to communicate with His Father, how much more do we? If *Jesus* needed the Spirit of God to open the heavens and make the realm of the invisible perceptible, how much more do we? If *Jesus* needed the Spirit of God to enable Him to hear the assurance of His Father's voice, how much more do we?

God doesn't want you to be limited to some theoretical, intellectual awareness that you are "in Christ." He sent His Spirit to live inside you to share a relationship with you on a very *personal* level. As a result, you can experience a deep-seated sense of belonging and confidence in God's unconditional love and acceptance.

As Paul wrote in Ephesians, "Long before he laid down the earth's foundations, he had us in mind, had settled on us as the focus of his love, to be made whole and holy by his love…Long before we first heard of Christ…he had his eye on us, had designs on us for glorious living, part of the overall purpose he is working out in everything and everyone" (Eph. 1:4,12, THE MESSAGE).

You are sealed by the Spirit. You bear His signet. His distinctive mark of ownership. How wonderful this is! Let the words of the Father resound in your soul: *I am so pleased with you.*

Living in the Shallows

The dominant worldview of our western society is Rationalism. Rationalism relies on natural human reason for the establishment of truth. It proposes that we live in a box consisting of time, space, energy, and mass. Man relates to this world with his five senses— his ability to taste, touch, smell, see, and hear. In this worldview, logic and analytical reasoning are regarded as superior to intuitive perceiving and sensing. Ideas based on information gleaned outside of our five senses or scientific investigation is viewed by Rationalism as questionable and inferior.

Rationalism has influenced and conditioned many of us in ways that have not promoted spiritual growth or cultivated an appetite for experiential encounters with the living God. Many of us have become rational Christians skilled in human reasoning, rather than spiritual Christians who confidently function in the spirit realm. We allow the spirit of the world to govern our lives more than the Spirit of God. We live in the shallows of the visible, rather than actively pursuing God and inviting the Spirit to tutor us in the domain of the invisible. And we miss out, never realizing our full spiritual inheritance in Christ.

The Spirit of God wants to lead us out of the shallows into the deep things of God. Paul makes this very clear:

> No eye has seen, no ear has heard, no mind has conceived what God has prepared for those who love him but God has revealed it to us by his Spirit. *The Spirit searches all things, even the deep things of God* ... We have not received the spirit of the world but the Spirit who is from God, that we may understand what God has freely given us. This is what we speak, not in words taught us by human wisdom but in words taught by the Spirit, expressing spiritual truths in spiritual words.
>
> —1 CORINTHIANS 2:9–10,12–13, EMPHASIS ADDED

In some ways I think it may have been easier to live by faith in the days of the early church. These saints *knew* their faith was anchored in the unseen. With their sights fixed on their invisible God, they rocked their world. These New Testament believers were not heavily influenced by the deification of logic and reason. Virtually half of the stories following Christ's death and resurrection are accounts of individuals who experienced direct encounters with the Spirit of God. They heard God speak to them. They had vivid dreams and visions. They saw images and pictures in the spirit realm. They sensed God prompting and leading them in specific directions. They witnessed His healing power flow through them when they ministered to those in need.

Many of these believers had walked and talked with Jesus during His three-and-a-half-year ministry on earth. They witnessed the miracle-working power of the Spirit flow through Him. The blind received sight. Cripples walked. Diseases disappeared. The delivered danced free.

I can't imagine what it must have been like when the disciples learned Jesus was going to leave them. They must have had hundreds of questions about the events Jesus warned them would happen.

I love the way Jesus addressed their fears:

> I will ask the Father, and he will give you another Counselor, who will never leave you...No, I will not abandon you as orphans—I will come to you.
> —JOHN 14:16,18, NLT

The word *orphans* in the original language brims with meaning. It carries a sense of hope not only for those who are bereft of parents, but also for students who have been abandoned by their teacher. The Holy Spirit lives in us to teach us, just as He taught the early disciples after the resurrection. His Spirit lives in us to tutor us in our relationship with God. He wants to assist us in our quest to go deeper.

Ephesians Meet the Holy Spirit

The Ephesians knew exactly what Paul was talking about when he reminded them that they were "sealed with the Holy Spirit of promise" (Eph. 1:13, NKJV). It had only been a matter of years since Paul first arrived in Ephesus. Rolling into town, the apostle found a group of believers who knew virtually nothing about the Holy Spirit. Upon hearing and believing the claims of Christ, this group had learned through John the Baptist that an experience with the Holy Spirit would come. John told them, "I indeed baptize you with water unto repentance, but He who is coming after me is mightier than I, whose sandals I am not worthy to carry. He will baptize you with the Holy Spirit and fire" (Matthew 3:11, NKJV).

The believers in Ephesus did not know that the Holy Spirit had come on the day of Pentecost. Realizing the gap in their understanding, Paul led them into an experiential encounter with the third Person of the Trinity.

And it happened, while Apollos was at Corinth, that Paul, having passed through the upper regions, came to Ephesus. And finding some disciples, he said to them, "Did you receive the Holy Spirit when you believed?" So they said to him, "We have not so much as heard whether there is a Holy Spirit." And he said to them, "Into what then were you baptized?" So they said, "Into John's baptism." Then Paul said, "John indeed baptized with a baptism of repentance, saying to the people that they should believe on Him who would come after him, that is, on Christ Jesus." When they heard this, they were baptized in the name of the Lord Jesus. And when Paul had laid hands on them, the Holy Spirit came upon them, and they spoke with tongues and prophesied.

—ACTS 19:1–6

I want to underline a critical truth here. If you have said yes to Christ, you *have* received the Holy Spirit. He lives *in* you. He signed, sealed, and delivered you into God's family. By "sealing," once again, I mean He marked you as His own. It was tantamount to saying, "This one's *Mine!*"

The phrase "baptism in the Holy Spirit" has been the source of much confusion and contention. In some circles, this biblical term has been vilified. This has likely occurred in reaction to groups who have misrepresented the biblical meaning of the word—or used the term as some sort of spiritual status symbol.

Some who say they are baptized in the Holy Spirit carry an air of self-appointed superiority, viewing themselves as Christ's elite—sort of a Christian-and-a-half. This stance is completely contrary to the nature and heart of God. A spirit of pride drives "spiritual elitism" and—watch out!—God hates pride. His Spirit strives against it. *The more you are filled with the Spirit of God, the more you will reflect a spirit of humility.*

There are seven references in the New Testament to the baptism *in* or *by* the Holy Spirit (Acts 19:1–6). Six of the seven verses refer to the baptism John the Baptist promised Christ would bring, fulfilled on the day of Pentecost. Nowhere in Scripture do we find the command for followers of Christ to be baptized in the Holy Spirit after the day of Pentecost. Nowhere in Scripture do we find that believers are told to pray for the baptism of the Holy Spirit after Pentecost. Paul does, however, command us to be *filled* with the Spirit.

Under the inspiration of the Holy Spirit, the apostle cried out for you and me, praying, "that you may be filled with all the fullness of God" (Ephesians 3:19). Receiving all the fullness of God could never happen in a single post-conversion experience. Being Spirit-filled does not stop with one divine encounter. Growing in the fullness of God happens in the context of an ongoing, life-long, interactive process.

+ I surrender my will and ask for His will.

+ I exchange my dreams for His dreams.

+ I lay down my perspectives and ask for His wisdom.

+ I offer God my weakness and open my life to His power.

+ I admit my timidity and receive His boldness.

God lavishes His blessings on those who are His. When those who have been sealed by heaven—those who bear the impress of His royal ring—ask, they are sure to receive (John 16:24).

One of the nineteenth century's mightiest men of God was Dwight L. Moody. Not only was he the founder of the Moody Bible Institute, but he was also an international teacher of the Bible. Hundreds of thousands of people came to know Christ under his teaching. Those who knew Moody said that one of the most noticeable characteristics of his life was that of total surrender to God. Every ounce of his two-hundred-eighty pound frame belonged to God. He wasn't perfect. He was surrendered. Dwight Moody's successor, R.A. Torrey, speaks of Mr. Moody's intense hunger for God, and of one of the divine encounters he had with the Holy Spirit:

> The first month I was in Chicago, we were having a talk about something upon which we very widely differed, and Mr. Moody turned to me very frankly and very kindly said: "Torrey, if I believed that God wanted me to jump out of that window, I would jump." I believe he would. If he thought God wanted him to do anything, he would do it. He belonged wholly, unreservedly, unqualifiedly, entirely, to God. Henry Varley, a very intimate friend of Mr. Moody once said to him: "It remains to be seen what God will do with a man who gives himself up wholly to Him." I am told that when Mr. Harley said that, Mr.

Moody said, "I will be that man."

In his early days Moody was a great hustler, he had a tremendous desire to do something but he had no real power. He worked very largely in the energy of the flesh. But there were two humble Free Methodist women who used to come over to his meetings in the YMCA. One was Auntie Cook and the other Mrs. Snow. These two women would come to Mr. Moody at the close of his meetings and say: "We are praying for you." Finally, Mr. Moody, being somewhat nettled said to them one night: "Why are you praying for me? Why don't you pray for the unsaved?" They replied, "We are praying that you may get the power."

Mr. Moody did not know what that meant but he asked that he might pray with them and not they merely pray for him. Auntie Cook once told me of the intense fervor with which Mr. Moody prayed on that occasion. She told me in words that I scarcely dared repeat, though I have never forgotten them.

Not long after that, he was walking up Wall Street in New York in the midst of the bustle and hurry of that city, and his prayer was answered. The power of God fell upon him as he walked up the street and he had to hurry off to the house of a friend and ask to have a room by himself. In that room he stayed alone for hours; and the Holy Ghost came upon him filling him with so much joy that at last he had to ask God to withhold His hand, lest he die on the spot from joy."[4]

Jesus said, "Blessed are those who hunger and thirst for righteousness, for they will be filled" (Matt. 5:6). The loving Father that He is, God loves to fill His hungry and thirsty kids. He is the lavish giver of all good gifts. Are you open to receive from Him today?

Here I am, Oh Lord, imprinted by Your seal of grace. Sometimes it is hard for me to see Your imprint of love on my life. Open my eyes Lord to new dimensions of Your power in me. Fire of the Holy Spirit, fall on me and consume that which is not of you inside my heart. Jesus, I surrender all of my life to You. I hold nothing back. Let Your sovereign plan be fully expressed in my life. Take me deeper—so much deeper, I pray. Amen.

CHAPTER 2

THE ONE WHO REVEALS

Pam Vredevelt

*T*HE HOLY SPIRIT is here with you right now. You are reading about Him in a book, and He is looking over your shoulder. There is not a corner in all the earth where He is absent (Ps. 139:8–10). He is present at all times, in all places, revealing God to you. When Christ is your Lord, your heart becomes His residence. He promised to come and make His home within you. And when He comes, He doesn't come to visit. He comes to set up housekeeping (Eph. 2:22).

Scripture speaks of the Holy Spirit as the "Spirit of wisdom and revelation" (Eph. 1:17–18). And it is this Spirit of wisdom who yearns to help you connect with God, the source of all understanding about every detail of your life. He can show you how to put principles of healthy living into practice, and empower you to act on what He shows you. I like the way J. B. Phillips paraphrased that thought in Philippians 2:13: "For it is God who is at work within you, giving you the will and the power to achieve his purpose."[1]

God promises a liberal outpouring of wisdom whenever you ask (Eph. 1:7–8). And what does *revelation* mean? The word *revelation* is used two ways in the Bible. The sixty-six books of the Scriptures are "the revealed Word of God." And this completed revelation is the solid ground upon which we build our lives, as Jesus made clear in His story about the wise man and the foolish man and the places they chose for home sites (Matt. 7:24–27).

But there is a second use of the term *revelation* in Scripture. The second usage refers to the Holy Spirit's work of unveiling the eyes of your heart to perceive what God wants to show you. The Spirit's passion is to help you know God better and to understand His purposes and power in your life. The Spirit of revelation opens the eyes of your heart to see what God wants to reveal to you (Eph. 1:17–18). He gives you insight, showing you how God is working in you and through you.

Knowing Above Reason

Oswald Chambers once wrote: "The Spirit of God takes the words of Jesus out of their scriptural setting and puts them into the setting of our personal lives."[2] A. W. Tozer elaborated further on the revealing work of the Spirit: "When the Spirit illuminates the heart, then a part of the man sees which never saw before; a part of him knows which never knew before, and that with a kind of knowing which the most acute thinker cannot imitate. He knows now in a deep and authoritative way, and what he knows needs no reasoned proof. His experience of knowing is above reason, immediate, perfectly convincing and inwardly satisfying."[3]

Apart from the indwelling Holy Spirit, we can't sense God's presence or discern His fingerprints on the situations of our lives. Human nature disconnected from God is in the dark, blind to the revelations of the Holy Spirit. It is the Holy Spirit who removes blinders and enlightens (2 Cor. 3:13–18, 4:4).

He is the One who reveals God and speaks to your heart of God's unconditional love for you. I've spoken with many spiritual seekers who believe in a god, but who are unclear about how Jesus

Christ does or doesn't fit with their "spirituality." In an effort to prompt them further in their search for God, I've asked, "If there is a God who loves you unconditionally, and who wants to have a friendship with you, would you be interested in knowing Him?" Some say no, they wouldn't. Others respond with a skeptical, "Um...maybe." But most acknowledge a genuine desire to know God in a personally relevant way.

That being said, I've offered this suggestion: "Get a Bible that's easy for you to read—one that uses words that make sense to you. Read the Book of John in the New Testament. As you read, ask the God who created you to reveal Himself to you."

I offered that challenge to Jim, an inquisitive young graduate student who knew nothing about the Bible or church. He had grown up in a family that never spoke of God or religion. Although he was an intelligent, accomplished musician, he complained of a dark void in his soul and thought he was depressed.

After several counseling sessions with this young man, it seemed likely that Jim wasn't suffering clinical depression. He was suffering intellectual disillusionment and searching for meaning and purpose in life. He realized something was missing, he just wasn't sure what.

One afternoon Jim entered my office and promptly informed me that he and his friends had gone to his favorite pub the night before. After pouring out his woes to his friends while downing a few pitchers of ale, his roommate declared in a drunken stupor, "Hey man—you need to try God!" It made Jim think.

And yes, I do believe the Holy Spirit can speak through an inebriated friend! The Holy Spirit is the most loving person you will ever meet. He is stubborn in His love for you. He will use anything, anywhere, at any time to draw you deeper into relationship with Him. If He will open the mouth of a donkey to help someone see the light, He can speak through a buddy who has had a few too many beers (Num. 22:28).

A few days after that bar scene, I listened to Jim philosophize over ideas he had picked up from a handful of religious sources. Toward the end of our session I asked if he was open to investigating something different. He agreed and accepted my challenge. A few weeks later he returned, having read the Book of John from beginning to end, twice.

Sitting forward on the edge of the couch, he held out a brand new Bible in midair and said, "Something flipped on the lights for me. I *get* it. It's all about Jesus!"

The blinders were off. The eyes of his heart were opened. The revelation of Jesus in the Scriptures became understandable. In his own way, with his own words, he said yes to Jesus and the light consumed the dark void within him. I later had the joy of opening the Bible with Jim and showing him it wasn't a "something" that had flipped on the lights for him. It was a Person—the Person of the Holy Spirit. The Spirit of revelation had enlightened him about Jesus and His gift of eternal life (Eph. 1:18–19). The moment he opened the door of his heart to Christ, the Spirit came to live within him.

It's always fun to show someone Revelation 3:20 for the first time: "Look! Here I stand at the door and knock. If you hear me calling and open the door, I will come in, and we will share a meal as friends" (NLT).

God doesn't want you to simply know about Him. He wants you to know Him personally and intimately, heart to heart, like very best friends (John 15:13–18). Everything about God is relational. Before Jesus completed His mission on earth, He spoke of His deep love for you, and promised to send the Holy Spirit to help you experience deep friendship with God.

> As the Father has loved me, so I have loved you. Now remain in my love…Greater love has no one that this, that he lay down his life for his friends. You are my friends if you do what I command. I no longer call you servants, because a servant does not know his mater's business. Instead, I

have called you friends, for everything that I learned from
my Father I have made known to you.
—JOHN 15:9, 13–15

It is to your advantage that I go away; for if I do not go
away, the Helper will not come to you; but if I depart, I
will send Him to you...I still have many things to say to
you, but you cannot bear them now. However, when He,
the Spirit of truth, has come, He will guide you into all
truth; for He will not speak on His own authority, but
whatever He hears He will speak; and He will tell you
things to come. He will glorify Me, for He will take of what
is Mine and declare it to you. All things that the Father has
are Mine. Therefore, I said that He will take of Mine and
declare it to you.
—JOHN 16:7, 12–15, NKJV

Jesus said, "Whatever He [the Spirit] hears He will speak"
(John 16:13, NKJV). This communication happens Spirit to spirit,
Friend to friend. It is engaging, lively, and interactive. Fellowshiping
with the Holy Spirit is truly the most magnificent of all the heavenly treasures we've been given. Nothing this world has to offer can
satisfy you like going into deeper levels of fellowship with God.
Nothing. Not money. Not prestige. Not power. Not anything.

You are created in God's image and designed for a love relationship with Him. From the moment you were born God has
been pursuing you, aggressive in His love, with whispers, shouts,
and silence. He orchestrates people and situations to intercept
you, tenaciously trying to captivate your attention and draw you
close. God says, "I have loved you, my people, with an everlasting
love. With unfailing love I have drawn you to myself" (Jer. 31:3).
The passionate cry of God's heart towards you has always been
and will always be, "Come to Me...Abide in me." (See Matthew
11:28; John 15.)

Please hear me, my friend: *As surely as He calls you into a saving knowledge of Christ, He calls you into the depths of Christ.*

THE ONE WHO REVEALS | 33

"God, I Want to Know You"

When we ask God to reveal Himself to us, the Holy Spirit will answer this prayer. He must be true to who He is—the agent of all revelation.

I spoke recently with a woman who was raised in a wealthy, militant Muslim family in Pakistan. By the time Karenze was twelve years old, she prayed religiously five times a day, prostrate on the floor. In spite of her deep devotion and consistent practice of spiritual disciplines, Karenze told her mother that her heart felt dead. She longed for the passionate spirit she saw in her religious leaders. Her mother advised her that she could find this spirit by going to one of the more prominent mosques in a nearby city.

Karenze made the trip with high hopes, only to crash deeper into despair after returning home.

The night following this spiritual journey, she locked herself in her bedroom, and in gut-wrenching anguish cried out: "Whoever you are, God, I want to know You. I'm calling on the Creator of the universe; the Creator of me; the God who made the stars and the mountains; The God who made this body that I live in."

As these words hit the air, it was as if someone opened her ears to the spirit realm. She heard conversations all around the room of frantic voices arguing, vying for her attention shouting, "What? What god? Who? STOP! Who are you talking to? The creator of what?" Again she cried out: "I want to know the Creator of the universe. The God who made me."

Immediately a loving presence filled her bedroom, silenced the voices, enveloped her with peace, and spoke one word to her: "Jesus."

She had never heard this word. "What is Jesus?" she wondered. Bolting from her room she searched for her father, the spiritual head of the household, certain he would know the answer.

"Father," she said, "what is Jesus?" He suddenly slapped her so hard it nearly knocked her off her feet. "You are to *never* speak that name again!" he snarled.

Shamed and stunned, Karenze locked herself in her bedroom, curled up in a fetal position on her bed, and cried: "Jesus! Jesus! Jesus! Who are You?"

Her sobs stopped abruptly when a man dressed in white appeared at the base of her bed. In the most kind and loving voice she had ever heard, He said, "I will never leave you, Karenze."

From that moment on, Karenze confidently believed that the personal presence of her Creator was with her wherever she went. Down deep in her heart, she knew that the man who appeared was "the Spirit of Jesus Christ." (See Philippians 1:19; Galatians 4:6; Romans 8:9.)

Karenze hid the encounter in her heart, telling no one, for fear of losing her life. A year later, while attending a university in India, Karenze "just happened" to meet an American woman in the community who was able to answer her questions about Jesus from the Bible. The more Karenze read God's written Word, the more God revealed Himself to her. She could not deny God's presence with her.

Six months later she turned her back on everything she had been raised to believe, and asked Jesus to be her Savior and Lord. At that moment, the Spirit of the living God invaded her soul, resurrecting her deadened heart to new life. As expected, Karenze's family cut off all contact with her and declared her dead. During the last eleven years several attempts have been made on her life. When I asked Karenze how she copes with the continual death threats, in an undaunted, matter-of-fact manner, she replied, "Persecution is a given. The darkness doesn't like the light. I am so blessed to know Christ."

"I Will Pour Out My Spirit"

Karenze cried out during childhood for an experiential knowledge of God that human wisdom and religious practices couldn't deliver. She desperately needed the Spirit to do what He does best. She needed Him to reveal God. Human nature, apart from the Spirit of God, does not understand the things of the Spirit. In fact, what the Holy Spirit reveals can seem downright foolish, even detestable to the natural mind.

Here is how Paul described it:

> When we tell you this, we do not use words of human wisdom. We speak words given to us by the Spirit, using the Spirit's words to explain spiritual truths. But people who aren't Christians can't understand these truths from God's Spirit. It all sounds foolish to them because only those who have the Spirit can understand what the Spirit means.
>
> —1 CORINTHIANS 2:13–14, NLT

Perhaps when you hear stories of others' experiences with God you feel a bit lost. Your mind keeps telling you that "things like that" happen to other people, but not you. Maybe you've concluded that you aren't capable of experiencing God up close and personal. Unfortunately, many Christians acquiesce to living in the shallows, thinking a deeper life with God is for a select few—or doesn't belong to this era of church history at all. Nothing could be further from the truth.

God offers the promise of His Spirit to everyone: "I will pour out my Spirit on *all* people. Your sons and your daughters will prophesy, your old men will dream dreams, your young men will see visions" (Joel 2:28, emphasis added). Peter preached this promise from the Old Testament Book of Joel shortly after Christ was raised from the dead and ascended to heaven. To those living in Jerusalem, his message was clear and simple:

+ Jesus is the crucified, resurrected, and exalted Lord and Christ (Acts 2:22–36, 3:13–15).

+ Jesus, who now sits at the right hand of the Father in heaven, has the authority to pour out the Holy Spirit on all believers (Acts 2:16–18, 32,33).

+ If you place your faith in Jesus as Lord and repent of your sin, you will be forgiven, and times of refreshing will come (Acts 2:36–38, 3:19).

+ As a believer, you can expect the gift of the Holy Spirit to be poured out on you, and on all generations after you (Acts 1:4–8, 2:38–39; Matt. 3:11).

God doesn't say, "I will pour out My Spirit only on a select few, the religious elite." Nor does He say, "I will pour out My Spirit for a few decades, until this generation of the early church passes away." God says, "I will pour out My Spirit on *all* people."

All means all—all nations, tribes, tongues, men, women, and eras. It also includes the good, bad, rich, poor, intellectual, and those with mental disabilities. When the Holy Spirit lives in you, He persistently draws you like a magnet, into the deep things of God, always pointing you to Jesus.

"Someone's Talking to Me"

My friend, the late Dr. Ron Mehl, related an incident about Diane, a young woman with Down syndrome, the daughter of a man in his church.

Diane, Dave Culver's daughter, lives in a group home in Salem, Oregon. Diane's mother was very ill, dying of cancer, and the situation was not improving. Dave decided to bring Diane home to Portland so she could visit her mom. After a short visit, Diane went back to Salem, but was very disturbed and emotional about the state of her mother's condition.

Upon arriving at the group home, Diane asked if she could meet with Mary, a professional counselor for disabled people.

Mary immediately noticed that Diane seemed troubled.

"What's wrong, Diane?"

"It's my mom," she answered. "I'm afraid my mother's going to die."

As Diane proceeded to talk to the therapist about her mom, she suddenly stopped, looked off into the distance, and a peaceful, serene look spread across her face.

"What is it, Diane?"

"Quiet!" she said, holding up her hand. "Someone's talking to me."

For a minute or so, not a word was spoken, and then the counselor finally asked, "Who is talking to you?"

"It was Jesus," Diane answered.

"What did He say?"

"He told me that He was going to take care of my mother and that everything would be all right."

From that moment on, Diane's demeanor changed. Her emotions were completely under control. Sometime later, Diane came back to Portland and was with the family when her mom, Anne, passed away. The night of the funeral, the house was filled with people. There were people sleeping everywhere, so they put a cot in her dad's room and Diane slept there. About 2:30 in the morning Diane woke up, rose from the bed, and opened the door to the bedroom. Dave woke just in time to see her coming back into the room. He gently asked her what was wrong.

"I saw a bright light," Diane replied. "I thought someone left the TV on in the other room."

Dave was puzzled. Everyone was asleep; there was no TV, and no light on anywhere in the house.

"What light?" Dave asked.

She looked at her dad and said, "It was Jesus. He told me that Mom's with Him now and that she's just fine. He said she was His to take care of."

With that, Diane went back to bed and quickly fell asleep.

People sometimes fabricate stories, create incredible plots, just for publicity and attention. But the young woman had no motive to create such a fantasy. Even her counselors, who are not Christian, said there was no way for her to stage a scene like that.*

One of the primary roles of the Holy Spirit is to reveal truth. Whatever He reveals will align with the written Word of God. Whatever He shows you will broaden your understanding and prompt you towards wisdom. When the Spirit shines His light in your heart, distorted perceptions of God fall by the wayside, and you see Him with greater clarity. He may also shine His light on specific areas of your life, granting you perspective that overrides human reasoning. Being the source of all knowledge, He may lovingly speak to you of things to come.

> But when he, the Spirit of truth, comes, he will guide you into all truth. He will not speak on his own; he will speak only what he hears, and he will tell you what is yet to come.
>
> —JOHN 16:13

These insights are always motivated by His kindness to benefit us.

"Oh God, Not That!"

When I was five months pregnant with our youngest son, Nathan, my husband, John, was driving his truck to the athletic club for his lunchtime workout. John loves to sing. And on this particular day he was listening to a CD and worshiping God at the top of his lungs. The sun had chased away the Portland clouds. John felt good. He looked forward to lifting weights and running some laps.

That's when it happened. In one world-stopping second, the

---

* Excerpted from *Angel Behind the Rocking Chair* © 1999 by Pam Vredevelt. Used by permission of Multnomah Publishers, Inc.

vivid picture of a little boy with Down syndrome flashed across the screen of his mind.

"Oh God," he breathed. "Not that. I couldn't handle that."

And just that quickly the reply came back, "You can handle anything I give you."

John hid that encounter with God in his heart for the next four months, uncertain if it was God revealing what was coming or his own worst fears surfacing. After Nathan was born, John told me the story and we both knew it had been the Holy Spirit who interrupted his worship in the truck that day. God was trying to get his attention to prepare him and give him confidence about what was to come.

Two months later, Nathan was born six weeks early, with a "surprise" diagnosis of Down syndrome and severe heart complications.

The cardiologist ran a battery of tests. Based on the results, he told us the center section of Nathan's heart was not formed and that he would need open heart surgery. During surgery he would construct the center portions of Nathan's heart so that he could oxygenate better and follow a more normal growth pattern.

Four days following that meeting, during the weekend services at church, Pastor Ted asked the congregation to join with him in a prayer for the healing of Nathan's heart. I received a call at the hospital that day from a woman in the congregation. She said that while the church was praying for Nathan, a picture came to her mind of a stream of blood flowing over Nathan's heart. As it passed over his heart, everything that was out of order was corrected and put in order.

She said to me, "Pam, the blood of Jesus has covered this problem. God is healing Nathan. Don't worry."

Numb with grief, I thanked her for the call, hoping the image she saw was imparted by the Spirit of God, and not the result of her own wishful thinking—or too many shots of espresso.

Two days later we took Nathan to see the cardiologist at

Emmanuel Hospital for more extensive testing. He wanted to examine all the cross sections of Nathan's heart on the ultrasound screen so he could determine how much of the heart muscle needed to be constructed.

We watched the screens intently as he focused on various chambers of the heart. When he got a clear shot of the center section, he started to shake his head and chuckle. I was not amused! Then in his clipped, British accent he happily announced, "By golly, the center of his heart is absolutely normal!" I burst into tears, grateful that Nathan didn't need open heart surgery.

I left the hospital that day with a renewed awareness: God is still in the business of healing and revealing whatever is in our best interest and for our highest good.

The Agent of Revelation

For me personally, Spirit-born revelations don't come as often as I'd like. This is probably because my efforts to draw near to God are frequently interrupted (James 4:8). God is always speaking, and I miss out on many of His life-giving words because there is too much busy noise in my life and I simply don't listen well (John 10:27). I've certainly learned through the years that what God says to me is far more important than what I say to Him.

The Holy Spirit is the agent of revelation. He peels away the veils that cloud your perception of who God is, and how God wants to share friendship with you in this world. He longs for you to draw near. He is passionate about taking you deeper in your experiential knowledge of the things that have been freely given to you by God. Paul tells us: "'No eye has seen, no ear has heard, no mind has conceived what God has prepared for those who love him,'—but God has revealed it to us by his Spirit" (1 Corinthians 2:9–10).

My guess is that you long to know God in a deeper way. Why else would you be reading this book? Perhaps you've asked yourself through the years, "How can I experience God at a deeper, more life-changing level?"

One answer is to simply spend more time seeking God, speaking to Him, and listening for His voice. God is more intimately present to you—with you, in you—than any human being can possibly be. As you fellowship with Him you will discover He is the most perfect and loving friend you will ever know. His thoughts are wise. His revelations transform.

Begin by reducing the noise in your life and setting aside time to be with the Lord. Turn off the phone. Turn off the TV. Find a quiet place, free from distractions, and turn your attention to Him. Take a few cleansing breaths and calm your mind. Ask the Spirit of wisdom and revelation to take the lead, and direct your desires to know God more deeply. Have faith, as the apostle James assures us, that when you draw near to God He draws near to you (James 4:8). Choose to believe what God says.

In the Quiet of His Presence

In a quiet place, in a quiet moment, read a brief passage from the Bible. The Scriptures will bring you to God. Read a few verses slowly, carefully, and reflectively. Talk with the Spirit while you are reading. Interact with Him. Ask Him to speak to you. Invite Him to show you what He wants you to see.

Our Lord asks us to watch and pray (Matt. 26:41). He doesn't ask us to do this to frustrate us. He asks us to do this so that He can satisfy our deepest needs. As you read the Scriptures, be sensitive to the spontaneous insights and images that bubble to the surface. *He will speak to you about your life.* Remember, you are reading to get close to your Lord, not for scholarly study. There are other times for that. In this quiet place you are intentionally engaging your spirit with God's Spirit to receive from Him.

Take time. Linger. Hush. Don't rush. Be still. Stillness enables you to know God (Ps. 46:10, 37:7). Quietness is a key to growing deeper. Wait in God's presence until you receive fresh perspective imparted by the Spirit of wisdom and revelation. Every time you draw near, He *will* come to you. He will meet with you. You will experience divine interchanges with God. Rivers of His love will flood your spirit, spilling over into your soul. Allow these life-giving waters to cleanse and refresh your mind, will, and emotions (John 7:37–39).

Forget the clock. Lose yourself in the depths of His infinite goodness. Abide with Him. Speak little. Listen much. Write down what you see and what you hear. The Holy Spirit will show you what you need to see to wisely navigate through the issues at hand. Whatever He reveals, He empowers. The insights He gives aren't simply to satisfy your curiosity. They are given to enable you to manage life well, with an unshakeable confidence that God is in you, working all things out according to His good pleasure. They are given to sustain you through chaos, direct you in decision, and comfort you in affliction. They impart life. If you want to go deeper with God, go to your heart. Human reasoning won't reveal God's perspectives, but His Holy Spirit will.

> *Dear Lord Jesus, the cry of my heart is to know You more. Take me deeper into You. Open the eyes of my heart to see You more clearly and to understand the plans and purposes You have for my life. Reveal Yourself to me. As I withdraw from the noise on the outside and commune with You, show me what You want me to see. Whisper words of wisdom to my spirit. Shine Your spotlight into my soul. Illumine the dark places. I abandon myself fully and completely into Your loving care. Spirit of wisdom and revelation, have Your way in me.*

CHAPTER 3

THE ONE WHO EMPOWERS

Pam Vredevelt

M Y HUSBAND, JOHN, loves being a pastor. Every now and then he visits people in prison. During one such visit he met an older, Hispanic woman, who was hunched over in severe pain. Her back had been bothering her for years, and there was a growth on the side of her head the size of an orange. Apparently the medical interventions offered in prison did not bring relief, and the woman wanted John to pray for her.

A young man, fluent in English and Spanish, offered to interpret for him. John gently laid his hand on the center of the woman's back, and asked God to touch her vertebrae and bring things into alignment. Suddenly, the woman became very excited and spouted off a string of words in Spanish, which the young man interpreted: "The lady says she felt heat down her backbone, and then it went pop-pop-pop. The pain is gone."

The woman was beside herself with joy, and then pointed to the growth on her head as if to say, "Okay, guys, get on with it, please. Finish the job."

When John laid his hand on the woman's head, the tumor filled the palm of his hand. He prayed for God's healing touch upon the woman and asked her to explain what she was sensing. As this was taking place, a group of prisoners began to gather around. It was obvious that their fellow inmate, who had been severely hunched over in pain, was standing up tall, pain free. They wanted John to pray for them, too.

Turning to the young interpreter, John said, "You keep praying for this woman while I pray for the others." The young man laid his hand on the tumor and began to pray the words he had heard John pray. (This was the first time this young man had ever prayed out loud for another person.) A few moments later, John's prayers were abruptly interrupted when the interpreter began jumping up and down, screaming at the top of his lungs, "It's gone! It's gone! It vanished! It's GONE!"

John examined the place where the tumor had been, and sure enough, there was no trace of it. The woman was beaming, and kept rubbing her head to make sure the lump was gone for good. This miracle was a sign from God for all the prisoners.

A sign is something that points beyond itself to something greater. This sign pointed to the healing power of the Lord Jesus Christ. John had the joy of sharing the good news of Jesus Christ and seeing many open their hearts to God's grace and forgiveness that day.

God of Miracles

God and miracles are inseparably linked. The Old Testament prophesied that the Messiah would usher in a kingdom characterized by the supernatural. The prophets testified of a coming day when people would experience spiritual and physical healings:

> Say to those who are fearful-hearted, "Be strong, do not fear! Behold, your God will come with vengeance, With the recompense of God; He will come and save you. Then the eyes of the blind shall be opened, And the ears of the

deaf shall be unstopped. Then the lame shall leap like a
deer, And the tongue of the dumb sing.
—ISAIAH 35:4–6

This promise reminds me of a little boy John met in Africa.
He and six team members went to help some others establish a
new church in Malawi village. Each morning they canvassed the
neighborhoods, inviting villagers to come to evening open-air
meetings where they could learn about Jesus.

As the team made its way through one corner of the village,
a crowd surrounded them. One of the team members noticed a
seven-year-old boy pushing his way through the crowd, trying to
grab the Scripture booklets from people's hands. Since the team
was low on supplies, the booklets were given only to the adults,
who were to read them to the children.

But this little guy was persistent. No, he was downright rude,
shoving and elbowing anyone who got in the way. When he finally
reached the team, several of the native women pointed to the boy
and said he had a demon. The boy had not spoken from birth.

The villagers weren't sharing this information as an interest-
ing fact. They were expecting John and the others to do something
for the boy. The group gathered around him, and one of the ladies
knelt down and talked to him about Jesus. The team laid hands on
him, told the demons to leave, and then helped the little boy invite
Jesus into his heart.

After the "Amen" the little boy hugged the Bible to his heart,
looked up at all the people around him and with tears in his eyes
spoke his first words, "Jesus loves me! Jesus loves me! Jesus loves
me!"

Word got around, and that night all the villagers from that
corner of town were at the crusade. Over 1,300 Malawi grandmas,
grandpas, moms, dads, and kids opened their hearts to Jesus.[1]

This isn't some third-hand story I've grabbed off the Internet.
This actually happened before my husband's eyes.

When you come across stories like these, do you find yourself thinking, *That happens to other people, not to me.* Do you have difficulty believing that God wants to work miracles in your life, too? Do you tend to forget that ALL things are possible with God?

I know I do. I fail to remember that the supernatural is natural for God. There are times when I completely overlook the fact that the Spirit of God, who dwells inside me, can:

+ Create something out of nothing

+ Radically change me and make all things new

+ Give me boldness and courage to speak in difficult situations

+ Energize me to persevere through crises and suffering

+ Give me divine perspective for making wise decisions

+ Keep me from falling to temptations that rob me of God's blessings

+ Heal me from sickness and disease

+ Deliver others and me from demonic influences

+ Work miraculous signs and wonders in the midst of my daily life.

Most of us have what I call "Oh, ye of little faith" moments, when our bewildered hearts cry out with the distressed father in Mark 9:24, "Lord, I believe; help my unbelief!" (NKJV).

Theology Takes a Wrong Turn

There are good reasons why we struggle to believe. During the 17th century, historians and philosophers began to assume that there was no place for the supernatural, miracle-working power of God. Some Protestant and Catholic theologians helped fan the flames of unbelief. The power and consistency of God was stressed in terms of immutable laws, set up by God to run the world. This kept God at a distance from the people, and pegged Him as One who was impersonal, and unavailable to intervene in the daily lives of men and women.

Miracles allegedly broke the unbreakable laws of nature, so in an effort to maintain coherency and logic, some philosophers and many scientists ruled miracles out of the picture. Skeptical historians encouraged us to doubt any claims of the miraculous. After all, if the laws of nature are virtually unbreakable, which is more likely—that a miracle has occurred, or that the observer is wrong or lying?

The dominant philosophies of current western society, rationalism and humanism, virtually slam the door on the supernatural, too, as Ted shared in an earlier chapter. The word *supernatural* refers to anything that occurs outside the normal experience or knowledge of man, and is not explainable by the known forces or laws of nature. These popular ideologies are skeptical of anything that lies beyond the scope of scientific investigation, intellectual reason, and our five natural senses.

While you are calculating the impact of these things, add the cynical and warped perspectives about God and Christianity that popular culture throws at us. The recently (and deservedly) cancelled NBC TV series, *The Book of Daniel*, was touted as a serious drama, featuring people who supposedly have a deep Christian faith. The program had nothing whatsoever to do with the biblical Book of Daniel, even though the series title would lead you to believe that it did.

The main character of the show was Daniel Webster, a drug addicted Episcopal Priest whose wife depended heavily on her mid-day martinis. The Webster family was rounded out by a twenty-three-year-old homosexual Republican son, a sixteen-year-old daughter who dealt drugs, and a sixteen-year-old adopted son who was having sex with the Bishop's daughter. At the office, Daniel's lesbian secretary was sleeping with his sister-in-law.

The mainstream media relished the prospect of this new drama, hailing the show "edgy, challenging and courageous."[2] *TV Guide's* Matt Roush lauded it as "darkly comedic and richly entertaining,"[3] while Robert Blanco of *USA Today* praised the show as "witty, earnest, intelligent...wildly entertaining and superbly cast."[4] The American public, however, "voted" on the program by simply turning it off, and the series went into the dumpster after just four episodes.

Acts of God?

I've also been struck how the media tends to categorize horrendous natural disasters as "acts of God." Really? How does God suddenly enter the picture? On all other counts many of them promote the godless concept that there is no cosmic plan, and that we exist in an impersonal universe controlled by natural laws. And when in comes to actual, bona fide demonstrations of God's supernatural power, the media does not deem them "newsworthy." Months of airtime and millions of dollars will be invested in anti-Christian programming like "The Book of Daniel," but rarely will we see news reports of how God is truly working in the world.

A recent survey by Princeton Survey Research Associates reveals that 90 percent of Christians believe in miracles, and 46 percent—almost half—of non-Christians believe in miracles.[5]

Since this is true, why are we so reluctant to talk about it? When was the last time you sat around a dinner table with a group of friends and heard someone say, "What has God been saying to you lately?" "What prayers has He answered this week?" "Tell us about the miracles He's done." "Who did God deliver?" "Who did He heal?" "How has He provided in supernatural ways?"

These topics are often pushed to the bottom of the list of conversation options, and I ask myself why. I suppose some of us were taught that it isn't polite to discuss politics, sex, and religion in public. Others of us learned in Sunday school that miracles "only happened during Bible times." We bought into the idea that supernatural signs and wonders have ceased, because those we respect said so. If we have never witnessed a true miracle, we may be slow to believe that they actually occur. As with Thomas after the resurrection, we doubt and want proof.

Perhaps you've seen a trend among the believers you know: We readily acknowledge our God as the One who parted the Red Sea, fed the masses with a few loaves of bread, and healed those who were crippled, diseased, and demonically influenced. And yet, somehow, our daily lives fall short of reflecting the truth that God's power is the same yesterday, today, and forever (Heb. 13:8).

Paul warned us about the teaching of spirituality without power:

> But mark this: There will be terrible times in the last days. People will be lovers of themselves, lovers of money, boastful...lovers of pleasure rather than lovers of God—having a form of godliness but denying its power.
>
> —2 TIMOTHY 3:1–5

Many speculate that we are living in the last days. Only God knows. But one thing is certain, this world is oppressed and deteriorating faster than any of us want to admit. If there was ever a time when mankind could benefit from God's supernatural power being asserted against the forces of sin, sickness, and Satan, the time is now.

The good news is, it's happening. God is raising up an army of believers who, with reckless abandon, are following Him into deep waters. Refusing to settle for a life of spiritual anemia, they cling to the deep conviction that the essence of who they are is spiritual, and that God wants to release the power of His Spirit through them. They're willing to risk, driven forward by a heart of compassion for the bruised and broken of this world. They're hungry to receive all the heavenly resources God wants to give them (Eph. 1:3).

As with those in the Book of Acts they are open to supernatural adventures with God through dreams, visions, and other divine encounters. They invite God to do the miraculous. They thrive on life-changing interactions with God. They stand in the gap for the oppressed, crying out for God's power to heal the brokenhearted and set the captives free. They pray expecting the Spirit of the living God to accomplish radical transformations in their lives, and the lives of others. They take Jesus at His word, believing that He meant what He said: "I tell you the truth, anyone who has faith in me will do what I have been doing. He will do even greater things than these, because I am going to the Father" (John 14:12).

This army of men and women, functioning in the power of the Spirit, are ordinary folks no different from you and me—imperfect people who struggle with a variety of problems, and wrestle with God over their doubts. Yet in the midst of it all, they seek God with all their hearts, choosing to boldly believe that He is who He says He is, and that He will do what He says He will do. They don't try to fulfill their life tasks without expecting God to demonstrate His power. They realize their spiritual poverty, cast aside all self-dependence, and earnestly seek God's supernatural empowering grace.

Here's the upshot of all this: God's power is being released in supernatural, mind-blowing, miraculous ways right smack in the middle of their ordinary, daily routines. Maybe that's at least part of what Jesus was talking about when He said, "Blessed are the poor in spirit, For theirs is the kingdom of heaven" (Matt. 5:3, NKJV).

Jesus, Our Model

The Scriptures prophesied that Jesus would come as an anointed healer and messenger of freedom and comfort:

> The Spirit of the Lord GOD is upon Me, Because the LORD has anointed Me To preach good tidings to the poor; He has sent Me to heal the brokenhearted, To proclaim liberty to the captives, And the opening of the prison to those who are bound.
> —ISAIAH 61:1, NKJV

When Jesus came, He ushered in the kingdom of God and fulfilled this prophecy (Luke 4:18–21). There are no recorded miracles during the first thirty years of Christ's life. It was after He was filled with the Holy Spirit that supernatural signs and wonders occurred. Wherever He shared the news of the kingdom of God, miracles happened.

> And Jesus went about all Galilee, teaching in their synagogues, preaching the gospel of the kingdom, and healing all kinds of disease among the people.
> —MATTHEW 4:23, NKJV

The people who lived and traveled with Jesus for several years witnessed His anointing with the Holy Spirit and with power. They saw Jesus going around doing good and healing all who were under the power of the devil. Christ's primary message was about the kingdom of God, a supernatural realm that exists within the heart of anyone who receives His gift of forgiveness. God's kingdom is not external, in the sense of being a political domain, it is internal and its essence is Spirit. Jesus taught His followers that they would be given the Spirit without limit (John 3:34).

Before leaving this world, He instructed them to wait in Jerusalem until they were "endued with power from on high." He made them a final promise: "But you shall receive power when the Holy Spirit has come upon you; and you shall be witnesses to Me" (Luke 24:49, Acts 1:8, NKJV).

The word power, *dunamis*, that Jesus uses here is the same word from which we get our word *dynamite*. It's a term depicting a mighty force of divine energy that can overcome all resistance. It's the same miracle working power Paul prays you and I will experience in our lives:

I pray also that the eye of your heart may be enlightened in order that you may know the hope to which He has called you, the riches of His glorious inheritance in the saints, and His incomparable great power (dunamis) for us who believe. That power (dunamis) is like the working of his mighty strength, which He exerted in Christ when he raised Him from the dead and seated Him at his right hand in the heavenly realms, far above all rule and authority, power and dominion, and every title that can be given, not only in the present age but also in the one to come (Eph. 1:18–21).

"For us who believe." Did you notice that pivotal phrase in the middle of the passage above? The power is for those who believe, not for those who don't believe. It's a Spirit-given power, ignited by faith and not human effort. Paul underlines this again in his letter to the church at Galatia:

> After beginning with the Spirit, are you now trying to attain your goal by human effort?...Does God give you his Spirit and work miracles [dunamis] among you because you observe the law, or because you believe what you heard?
>
> —GALATIANS 3:3,5

The answer is clear. Believing is the key. By faith, we receive the promise of the Spirit (Gal. 3:14). Incidentally, the words "give" and "work" in this text are present participles, which indicate a continuous, ongoing manifestation of God's supernatural miracle-working power.

So, where is this miracle-working power today? Why do so many believers look back on these things as historical events, rather than current realities? Why do some believers acknowledge the existence of the Holy Spirit, and yet not experience evidences of His power in their daily lives?

I can really only speculate. Perhaps they have not been taught about the Person of the Holy Spirit. Perhaps they don't know what the Bible says about who He is and how mighty He is in our lives. Perhaps they're simply too busy with other things to even think along these lines. Perhaps they make the assumption that God doesn't move in people's lives today as He did when Jesus was on earth.

One thing is certain: if we don't ask, we don't receive (James 4:2). This may be why Jesus told us repeatedly to ask.

> So I say to you, ask, and it will be given to you; seek, and you will find; knock, and it will be opened to you. For everyone who asks receives, and he who seeks finds, and to him who knocks it will be opened. If a son asks for bread from any father among you, will he give him a stone? Or if he asks for a fish, will he give him a serpent instead of a fish? Or if he asks for an egg, will he offer him a scorpion? If you then, being evil, know how to give good gifts to your children, how much more will your heavenly Father give the Holy Spirit to those who ask Him.
>
> —LUKE 11:9–13, NKJV

What Happened to Pastor Daniel?

Stories from around the world document the fact that when people ask, God responds. I surely wish the media would bombard the airways with these true-life accounts of God's supernatural power invading the earth. Wouldn't it be great to see the mocking nonsense of NBC's *Book of Daniel* pre-empted by a news flash telling the true story of Daniel Ekechukfwu, a Nigerian Pastor, who, after being dead three days, came back to life?

Relatives report that Pastor Daniel was in a serious car accident. Apparently his brakes failed, and he slammed into a concrete pillar. After being rushed to a Nigerian hospital and examined by doctors, he was transported to another hospital. While in route to the second hospital, he died.

The physician on duty, Dr. Josse Annebunwa, reports: "When I examined him, I looked at the chest, and there were no respiratory movements. I listened with the stethoscope and there were no breathing sounds. I searched the heart and cardiovascular system, and there were no sounds. The patient had no pulse. I looked at the eyes and the pupils were fixed and dilated. I concluded he was dead, and should be removed to the mortuary."

The mortician, Barlingon R. Mann said, "When Daniel's father and wife brought the body to the mortuary it was lifeless. There was no heartbeat and no signs of breathing. I accepted him as a corpse." For three days, Daniel's body lay on a slab in the mortuary awaiting his memorial service.

While waiting for the funeral, Daniel's wife bombarded heaven with her prayers. "I began to call on the name of the Lord," she reported. One verse that inspired her to pray for a miracle was Hebrews 11:35: "Women received back their dead, raised to life again."

Three days after Daniel's death, his wife went back to the mortuary, retrieved her husband's corpse, and transported it to a Christian prayer service being held by the evangelist, Reinhard Bonnke. One of the workers at the church told her, and those who were helping, to take the corpse to the basement. They laid the body across two tables, and several pastors began to pray for him.

One of the pastors recounted the following: "As we were praying, suddenly we saw the eyes start to move and life returning to the body." One pastor massaged the left hand, another the right. As they massaged where rigor mortis had set in, the area around his heart became hot and he began to breath.

Astonishing every one, Daniel jumped to his feet, and immediately asked for water. Stunned onlookers shouted, "Water! He's asking for water! Get him water!"

The news of Daniel's resurrection filtered up the stairs and out the door. People thronged to see the dead man sitting upright, talking with those surrounding him. The news of this astounding miracle spread like wildfire across Africa, and many trusted in the Lord Jesus Christ.[6]

Please grab on to what I say next. *It is the Holy Spirit who releases the power of God.* This was true for Jesus, and it's true for you and me (Luke 4:18; Acts 1:8, 10:38).

Scripture makes it very clear where the Holy Spirit does and does not release His power. We do not see the mighty release of God's power in human self-sufficiency, cleverness, wealth, or natural gifts. The Holy Spirit releases God's power most effectively in our weaknesses.

Most of us have a hard time wrapping our minds around this paradox of power in weakness. We prefer strength, competence, and a sense of control. We despise feeling powerless and vulnerable. But God delights in releasing His power through our frailties. Weak human beings are the best conduits of His power (2 Cor. 12:9–10).

The weaknesses you despise in your life are the very areas in which the Holy Spirit wants to equip you and exert His life-giving energy. Your weaknesses are the locations where God can most effectively display the excellence of His power (2 Cor. 4:7, 12:10).

I've seen it in my own life. Some of the greatest releases of God's power have come during times of crushing sorrow and overwhelming weakness. In the darkest nights He graced me with eyes of faith, enabling me to see and understand that which had been imperceptible to me before.

Power Out of Weakness

I recall a night about six months after our oldest daughter Jessie was in a bad car accident on the freeway. She was very sick with dizziness, nausea, and a chronic, debilitating headache. I was weary from the sorrow of watching her suffer through these bouts month after month with little change. She was in her junior year of high school and I was riddled with "what if's."

What if she doesn't get better? What if no one can help her? What if she can't graduate? My thoughts spun round and round with worst-case scenarios. I crawled into bed that night and cried myself to sleep. Now, years later, I can see how the Holy Spirit was working overtime that night to help me in my weakness (Rom. 8:26).

Around 3:00 a.m., I awakened. Strangely, my first waking thought was of a dream I'd had the summer before Jessie entered high school. How odd. I usually don't remember my dreams, but this one was different. In fact, it was so vivid I sat up and wrote it in my journal.

In the dream I saw Jessie standing in a cap and gown on the stage at high school graduation. She seemed happy and was saying something to the audience. What I heard in my heart puzzled me: "She will be fine. It will be a fight, and I will do the fighting for you."

The words were familiar. I had memorized a similar statement years before when studying the life of Moses. The Israelites were on their mass exodus out of Egypt and everything seemed to be going wrong. With the Red Sea before them and Egyptian warriors quickly closing behind them, the Israelites cried out to God in panicked desperation. Moses hushed the crowd and boldly declared: "Don't be afraid. Just stand where you are and watch...the Lord will rescue you...The Lord will fight for you, and you won't need to lift a finger!" (Exod. 14:13–14, TLB).

Even at the time, I believed the dream had been from the Lord. But I had just assumed God was giving me a heads-up that some adolescent challenges were on the way. He wanted to reassure me that He was going to be with us in the struggle, acting on our behalf. I couldn't have guessed what God was really preparing me for. I never imagined our story unfolding the way it did.

Going into high school Jessie was an "A" student. It never crossed my mind that I'd ever be worried about her potential to graduate.

But God knew. He woke me up one sorrowful night to remind me of an earlier dream, and underlined His words of promise: *She will be fine. It will be a fight and I will do the fighting for you.* His words became a source of renewal. His thoughts ignited power in my spirit that raised me out of a black hole of despair.

"Don't Grieve ... Trust"

One afternoon during Jessie's senior year, I was grieving over the physical and mental losses she had suffered due to the auto accident, gripped by fear about her future. In my journal I wrote: "God, I hate being in this place. It's dark and scary ..." I wrote several more paragraphs and then finished my thoughts with, "And on top of all that, I am sick of grieving!"

Relief came as I honestly expressed my feelings without censorship. After placing the period at the end of my last sentence, these words *passed* through my mind: *I don't want you to grieve, I want you to trust.*

The words hit me like the smack of a two by four. The Holy Spirit was giving me an assignment that seemed to contradict my clinical training and former life experience. After all, it's normal to grieve when we've lost something near and dear to us. But in the quiet of the moment, I knew my Father's voice, and His words were life to my soul. I've learned that there are times when God's directives don't line up with human reasoning, and that I had best pay attention to what God is saying. He wouldn't say it if He didn't intend to make it possible.

In the months following that encounter, I made a concerted effort to take a stance of trust, particularly when my heartache was more severe. On the days I felt like I was drowning in waves of sadness, I wrote in my journal: "Trust God, Pam. Trust God. He will do what He said He will do. He will do what you cannot do. Just trust Him."

Graduation day arrived. On her way out the front door, Jessie called out, "Bring the video camera tonight, Mom! I'm in a short drama that opens and closes the ceremony." Jessie paraded across the stage with the rest of her class, as family and friends whooped and hollered from the coliseum seats.

I had a hard time seeing through the camera lens that day. Tears welled without warning as I watched the dream I'd had four years earlier come to pass right before my eyes. There she stood, on stage, addressing the audience, just as God had shown me. He had seen her through and empowered all of us to endure a dark season of grief.[7]

It's more obvious to me now, years later, that time and again God's power resurrected me out of a bottomless pit of self-pity and depression. His strength supported me mightily in my weakness.

Life brings most of us to places where we realize we simply don't have the internal resources we need to handle the external pressures weighing on us. We lose confidence in our own efforts and abilities. These are the times when the Spirit of God will wow us with His wonders, if we will but turn and say, "I'm so weak. I need Your power. I can't do this on my own. Fill me with Your Spirit. Grace me with Your strength. Release Your supernatural power in this fragile heart of mine."

I want to be part of God's army in this generation. I want to be one of God's kids who believes big. I want to experience more of His resurrection power.

How about you? What wonders do you want to see God work in your life? What miracles would you like to witness in the lives of your loved ones? Who do you know that needs to hear about the Good News of Jesus? How about asking God to confirm the message of His grace with signs and wonders? (See Mark 16:17–18; Acts 14:3.) Let's join forces and make a bold decision to believe. Adventures in the Spirit await us.

Oh God, how I long to see You free to move in power through my life. So many are suffering and need Your healing touch. Cleanse me of anything that would hinder the flow of Your Spirit through me. Fill me to overflowing with a spirit of faith. Make me a conduit of Your miracle-working power. I want to believe You to work in BIG ways among my family, friends, and those with whom I cross paths. Sensitize me to hear the promptings of Your Spirit to pray for miracles. Empower me with courage to obey. Display Your wonders in this generation as You did in days of old.

CHAPTER 4

THE ONE WHO RELEASES

Ted Roberts

*I*PAUSED A MOMENT—JUST for a moment—before taking the plunge. Why had I paused? A flicker of warning, perhaps.

Gentle waves slapped against the side of our dive boat anchored in Chuuk Lagoon. Beneath the surface of these tropical deep-blue waters of the central Pacific Ocean, lay treasures of history awaiting our discovery.

Early in the morning of February 14, 1944, U. S. Task Force 58 launched a devastating attack on the Japanese fleet positioned in this lagoon. In nine relentless waves, more than four hundred fifty American fighter aircrafts swept over the Japanese forces, sending fifty Japanese ships to the ocean floor.[1]

Chuuk Lagoon had been considered an ideal, naturally protected harbor in the middle of Micronesia during World War II. Fifteen large islands, and a near-circular one-hundred-forty-mile barrier reef with five passages to the open sea, surround the lagoon. This perceived protection, however, made an escape next to impossible—and ultimately resulted in the demise of the powerful Japanese fleet.

History speaks, if we're willing to listen. Preparing to dive, I thought of times I had retreated into perceived "safe places" of my own making, only to end up feeling trapped and overpowered by enemy forces within and without. Only God's goodness and grace could have led me through the deep waters of my own private battles of the heart.

Taking a giant stride off the aft end of the dive boat, I hit the water and slowly descended. An explosion of bubbles engulfed me, dancing their way up to the surface. The rhythmic sound of my regulator filled my ears as I slowed my breathing, and finned into the depths.

Then, out of the abyss, she appeared. An amazing relic, the Shinkoku Maru, stretched five hundred feet from stem to stern. Her bridge was blanketed in hard and soft corals, flaunting their rainbow colors in our beams of light.

In its prime, this mighty vessel was a heavily armed fleet-oiler used in Admiral Nagumo's initial strike force on Pearl Harbor. The ship is one of many WWII wrecks scattered across seventy-seven square miles of ocean floor. Awed by the historic ghost fleet that lay beneath me, I paused momentarily to take it all in. I was entering a realm frozen in time.

I couldn't have known what the day would bring. I had no idea how close this "relaxing adventure" would bring me to eternity. But the Holy Spirit knew. He was about to teach me some profound lessons as I dove deeper than I had ever gone before.

Into the Depths

Most of us have places in our lives that are frozen in time. Don't be deceived; entering into a relationship with God doesn't automatically set everything straight in our soul. It takes time for God to work His chiropractic adjustments, realigning the places in our soul that have been out of alignment for years.

Deep, long-lasting change occurs as we move through life

with the Holy Spirit, experiencing consistent, ongoing interactions with God.

+ Interactions where He leads, and we follow.

+ Interactions where He initiates, and we respond.

+ Interactions where He instructs, and we obey.

He calls us out of the familiar shallows into deeper water than we've ever experienced before.

> When He had stopped speaking, He said to Simon, "Launch out into the deep and let down your nets for a catch."
>
> —LUKE 5:4, NKJV

In the context of these interchanges with the Spirit, surface things take on a whole new perspective. That's certainly the way things played out in Paul's life.

After a supernatural encounter with God on the road of Damascus, everything Paul had previously prized went by the wayside (Acts 9:1–22). After being knocked to the ground by the power of God, the only thing that really mattered to the former persecutor was growing deeper in his relationship with Christ. Public opinion, status, money, position, and personal power were no longer priorities. They didn't even show up on his radar.

There was no pompous air about Paul. No ivory towers. No aloof, I'm sharper and smarter and better-than-you attitude. On the contrary, he was a humble man, who called himself "a prisoner of Jesus Christ" (Eph. 3:1). A prisoner is someone who is captured and held captive. Had he wanted to, Paul could have chosen a number of different titles from his long list of impressive accolades and accomplishments. But he seemed to favor the word "prisoner," wearing it like the badge of honor it truly was.

History tells us Paul was one of the most educated and cultured men of his day. He attended the finest rabbinical schools and trained under Gamaliel, one of the most renowned rabbis of the first century (Acts 22:3). Paul was a brilliant multilingual, multitalented man. His countrymen touted him as a rising star in Judaism.

Until, that is, the moment he became a follower of Christ. After that, he was the laughing stock of the Jewish intelligentsia. Fellow rabbis must have thought Paul was smoking weeds from the fields when they heard him tell the masses that a Galilean carpenter was God.

None of that bothered Paul. He delighted in being identified as a prisoner of Christ, held captive by the forgiveness and grace of God. Boldly declaring himself the least of those who followed the Lord, Paul rejoiced over being chosen to declare God's unsearchable riches, the greatest of all treasures being Christ living in you (1 Cor. 15:9; Col. 1:27).

I have a picture hanging in my office at home that reminds me that I, too, am a prisoner of God's grace. It contains a pen and ink drawing of each aircraft I flew in the military—and a few medals I received for surviving the experience.

Whenever I glance at that picture, I'm transported back in time to an incident that happened the week after I committed my life to Christ in a bunker in Vietnam.

Alive By His Grace

During a night close air support mission, the troops on the ground were taking quite a beating. Our air support was called in to keep them alive.

My flight leader rolled in and dropped his bombs, precisely where the forward air controller had instructed him, and I was right on his tail. Distracted by the deadly fire being exchanged on the ground, I overshot the point of alignment from which I was to drop my bombs. In all my years of flying, I had never done that before. Without the proper alignment, bombs would land on our own troops. This is called "friendly fire."

The moment I was scheduled to roll in, hidden antiaircraft guns suddenly unleashed a flood of fire. It was obvious that the enemy had been monitoring conversations with the forward air controller and knew my location. I watched those fiery streams of death light up the night sky as they soared by, narrowly missing me. In the heat of the battle, I heard the Lord say to me as clearly as I have ever heard anything, "Ted, if you hadn't decide to follow Me last week, those bullets would not have missed. You are alive because of My grace."

A little of my arrogance melted away that night. Places in my soul that had been frozen for years began to thaw in the warmth of God's kindness. If you are struggling with the theological implications of this incident, it's probably not worth your energy. I stopped trying to figure it out long ago. All I know is that I am alive today by the grace of God. Like Paul, who pulled himself up off that dusty Damascus road, I am delighted to have been captured by God's grace. Believe me—the other option was not at all attractive!

I don't need position, title, or acclaim. I'm just thrilled to be alive, and I long to give Christ my very best.

When Paul speaks of being the least of those who follow Christ, he isn't talking from a bad case of low self-esteem. In the same breath he lays his life alongside the other apostles—a fairly impressive group of contemporaries—and declares, "I worked harder than all of them" (1 Cor. 15:10).

Those aren't the words of somebody with a lousy self-image. But Paul does speak, however, the language of brokenness and bold surrender. And that is precisely why we see the Holy Spirit move so powerfully in his life. He handed everything over to God (Rom. 12:1–2). He surrendered who he was in the past, and who he hoped to be in the future. He stopped giving orders, and started taking direction from the Holy Spirit, giving Him full access to his heart for His plans and purposes.

There are areas within all of our lives that must be confronted and boldly surrendered as we journey deeper in our experience with God. If this doesn't happen, we're simply playing religious games. And I must warn you. Going deeper with God isn't always an easy journey—which is precisely why so many folks tend to avoid it.

Paul tells us, "as many as are led by the Spirit of God, these are sons of God" (Rom. 8:14, NKJV). I have heard people quote that verse with a dreamy tone in their voice, as if to imply that the Spirit-filled life is some kind of love-boat cruise over tranquil, sunset seas.

A closer look at the original language quickly dispels that view. The word Paul chooses to describe the process, which we translate "led", is *ago*.[2] This is the root for the Greek word *agon*, from which we get the English word "agony."

Agon refers to an intense conflict, like we might see in a full-throttle, no-holds-barred wrestling match. It implies a violent struggle of the human will. Paul is clearly saying that when we are led by the Spirit, we will be prompted to deal with deep heart issues that block us from receiving His blessings. Don't think of an interstate freeway here; think of a steep mountain trail full of switchbacks. Ask anyone who has been a follower of Christ for several years, and they'll admit (if they're honest), that going deeper with God can feel like an agonizing tug-of-war at times (Rom. 6–8).

Spiritual growth pains are part of the long-term game plan. That's why Paul prays for you and for me, asking God that we might "be strengthened with might through His Spirit in the inner man" (Eph. 3:16, NKJV).

Sadly, some folks never invite God to help them with the deeper issues of their heart. They keep painful secrets locked inside, bury their feelings alive, and never expose their wounds to God's healing touch. The Holy Spirit isn't given the opportunity to do what only He can do. And the result? Many endure a lifetime without ever experiencing the depths of God's infinite love. They wet their toes in the foam at the edge of the surf and think they're swimming in the ocean.

No wonder so many throw in the towel on spiritual growth and conclude their faith "doesn't work"! Why bother with the perfunctory routine of going to church if you aren't experiencing the life-changing power of the Spirit in ways that truly make a difference?

By now I hope you are asking, "How does the Holy Spirit change, renew, and heal us deep within?" Now that's a great question! In fact it's such an important question that we're going to devote two chapters to the subject.

Transformation is not a simple process. I refer to it as a 3-D process. It is not one-dimensional. I often remind myself of this fact, especially when I'm stuck in the middle of a perplexing problem or overwhelming struggle. These truths help me keep my cool and put the skids on panic.

The truth is, the Holy Spirit knows you way better than you know yourself. (It isn't even close.) He loves you more than you love yourself. And He will lead you through changes of the heart that will cause you to stand in awe of His goodness and grace. If you could see a before and after snapshot, (who you are now, next to who you will become by God's transforming power) your jaw would hit the floor, and you'd be absolutely speechless.

Now listen carefully. Jesus Christ is our supreme example of how life can be lived in consistent communion with God. Jesus was guided and empowered—every moment of every day—by the Spirit who lived within Him. You and I have God's Spirit within us, as well, and He wants to give us everything we need to deal effectively with all the issues of our heart (2 Cor. 9:8; Phil. 4:19).

Here's the first "D" of the 3-D transformation process.

Deal With Your Hang-ups

We all have them. It doesn't matter if you were raised in church and never smoked, chewed, or went with girls or boys who do! Part of the price of living in a fallen world is the hidden snares that snag us, hook us, and trip us up. If you think you've never been snared, that's certain proof that you have. And the snare is pride!

Numerous passages in the Psalms speak of the traps, snares, and hidden nooses waiting to tangle and bind the people of God.

> My eyes are ever on the LORD, for only he will release my feet from the snare.
>
> —PSALM 25:15

> We have escaped like a bird out of the fowler's snare; the snare has been broken, and we have escaped.
>
> —PSALM 124:7

> Proud men have hidden a snare for me; they have spread out the cords of their net and have set traps for me along my path.
>
> —PSALM 140:5

The bottom line is that just because we're believers doesn't mean we don't have hang-ups to deal with. They're out there, ready to snag us if we don't walk carefully, day by day with Holy Spirit guidance.

During my dive in Chuuk Lagoon, I learned a valuable life lesson about hang-ups—literal and otherwise.

After several days of exploring the perimeter of the sunken ships, I wasn't content and wanted to see more. So I talked a young dive guide into taking me into the interior of one of the ships, even though I wasn't certified for that type of diving.

The group descended, enjoying the abundant array of tropical fish, anemones, gorgonians, and eagle rays, on the way to the bottom. As planned, the guide sought me out before the dive ended and motioned query—did I want to see inside the wreck? My dive computer said I was low on air, but I thought, Why not? This is a once in a lifetime experience. I'll just take a peek. A few minutes won't hurt.

I followed my friend into a pitch-black environment where few of the visual cues made sense. The ship was on its side, the interior a jumbled mess. Ceilings and floors had exchanged places. We squeezed our way around and through twisted pipes, catwalks, and odd debris strewn throughout this nautical relic. Visibility was poor, and every movement seemed to stir up silt. The narrow beam of my dive light barely revealed the fins of the guide in front of me. As we continued deeper, a tiny alarm bell sounded in my mind. My air supply! It was down to a razor-thin margin.

No sooner had that thought crossed my mind when another diver exploded past me, nearly knocking off my mask and regulator, as he frantically sought for a way out. In his haste he kicked up sixty years worth of silt inside the ship's compartment, reducing visibility to zero. Worse yet—when I tried to move forward, I couldn't. My tanks were hung up on something I couldn't see or reach, and started to panic. The strangest thought crossed my mind, *If I die down here, my wife is going to kill me!*

Intense stress-filled situations have a distinct way of revealing our hang-ups. As I struggled against whatever was preventing my forward movement, I asked myself: *Ted what drove you to do this? Why are you so compelled to push the limits?*

Have you ever thought about the drives in your life? The strongest drive you have is to breathe. The sheer intensity of that drive grabbed me by the throat in the dark entrails of that dead ship. I don't care how nice you are or how spiritual you are, if someone or something blocks your ability to get air, you will take action. We have other innate physical drives—the need for water, food, and sleep. God has also created us with needs for safety, loving relationships, and for finding and fulfilling our God-given purpose in this world.

Scientists tell us that our physical drives are governed by a part of the brain known as the hypothalamus. This little portion of gray matter monitors all of our bodily functions, and strives to maintain a state of balance called homeostasis. It functions somewhat like your thermostat at home, which regulates the comfort zone between a high and low setting. The midrange between the two extremes is where you find balance and normality.

Where am I going with this? Our innate drives are natural. It is not wrong to need air, water, food, love, or a sense of significance. The problem lies in the fact that all the normal settings on our drives have been corrupted by sin. The apostle Paul wanted to make sure we understood this. In Romans 5:12, he wrote: "When Adam sinned, sin entered the entire human race. Adam's sin brought death, so death spread to everyone, for everyone sinned" (NLT).

Just as a computer virus corrupts a hard drive, distorting its ability to process information correctly, so sin corrupts the human heart. This corruption leads us to try to meet legitimate needs in unhealthy ways. Following our natural impulses, we entertain and nurture jealousy, envy, bitterness, rage, lust, and immoral thoughts and actions.

Scripture is clear about this:

> Now the mind of the flesh [which is sense and reason without the Holy Spirit] is death [death that comprises all the miseries arising from sin, both here and hereafter]. But the mind of the [Holy] Spirit is life and [soul] peace [both now and forever].
>
> —ROMANS 8:6, AMP

Our natural drives, apart from the influence of the Holy Spirit, set us up to get hung up. James opens our eyes to the process:

Everyone is tempted by his own desires as they lure him away and trap him. Then desire becomes pregnant and gives birth to sin. When sin grows up, it gives birth to death.

—JAMES 1:14–15, GWT

Please notice the sequence here. It starts with a desire. Lured away, we bite the bait. Sin happens, and then something in our heart dies.

Setting the Hook

Several years ago I was asked to speak at a leadership conference in Jackson Hole, Wyoming. The cabins were primitive but I was told the fly-fishing was world-class. Early one morning I tried my luck with some borrowed gear. The scenery was stunning, like something right off a picture postcard. But my fishing? Well, let's just say it was not picture-perfect. I was doing little more than getting my lure wet.

As I worked diligently at my cast, I noticed a fisherman downstream hauling out one trout right after another. What in the world was his secret? Humbling myself, I waded down to him and asked if he would help me. That expert fly fisher taught me two things that day I'll never forget. First, he said, "Carefully watch the trout feed. They'll go for insects local to the stream or nearby fields. Select a lure that looks like what they're feeding on."

He picked a fly out of my tackle box, and tied it ever so masterfully onto my line. His knot looked nothing like the fifty-pound granny knot I had tied. Handing the rod back to me, he smiled and said, "Now—give it a try."

On my second cast, the water exploded when a huge trout hit the fly. Instantly I started reeling in the fish. My friend quickly advised me to try a different approach. (And that was the second lesson.) Taking my reel in hand, he kept a slight tension on the line and let it play out. Like a good coach, he explained the reason behind the method: "You have to let the trout wear himself out to set the hook."

I thought to myself, *I can't believe this guy. He's just like the devil!*

You see, our spiritual adversary studies us very carefully. He is not omniscient, but he has a keen memory. And he knows what we "feed" on. He takes note of all the desires that drive us and strategically places bait in front of our nose. If we don't bite the first time, he will recast another lure, and send it our way...and another...and another. Noticing the bait, we may think, "I'm a believer. I can't do that," to which the devil responds, "Aw, go ahead. It won't hurt anything. No one's watching."

Lured away from our convictions we bite the bait and find ourselves hooked. One of the devil's deadliest games is tempting us to meet legitimate needs in unhealthy ways. He works overtime to deceive us into believing that something bad is something good (1 Tim. 4:1). The booming industry of pornography is one good example.

But let's be straight about this. The devil is a liar, influencing us to exchange the truth of God for lies. Jesus referred to him as "the father of lies," and warned us to be on guard against his deceptions (John 8:44, NLT). He masterfully orchestrates circumstances, tantalizing us to take his bait. Then, amused by our torment, he waits until just the right moment to set the hook deep.

Now, back to my dive into the sunken ship. Time was running out. I was low on air and unable to shake myself loose. I couldn't see what I was hooked on, but knew something had to happen fast for me to come out of the dive alive. As my life flashed before my eyes, I wondered what had driven me to push the limits, one more time. Believe me, God had my undivided attention! I was trapped and powerless. The harder I struggled, the worse things got. And every ounce of exertion demanded more of my dwindling air supply.

That brush with death at the bottom of Chuuk Lagoon was a snapshot of my life. So often I've tried to strive, drive, and power my way through entanglements of the heart, only to end up exhausted and more defeated. For too many years I pulled myself up by the bootstraps and pushed ahead in life, while ignoring the pain in my soul that was screaming for attention—pain related to the wounds I suffered long ago, when I was just a boy.

The good news is, when we go deeper with God, He goes deeper with us. There is no hook so deep that the Holy Spirit can't reach and remove (1 Chron. 28:9; Ps. 7:9; Jer. 17:10). He sees all, knows all, delivers, and heals. He specializes in laser-pointing our deepest needs, and showing us how to remove one painful barb at a time. As we follow His lead, He skillfully and thoroughly transforms us from the inside out (2 Cor. 3:18). But, as I said earlier, the journey isn't always easy.

"You Want Me to WHAT?"

One morning I was preparing a teaching about the love of Father God for our church family. Out of the blue I sensed the Holy Spirit say, Ted, I want you to thank Me for your father.

I can't express how shocked I was by those words. "You want me to what?" I blurted out. "I want you to thank Me for your father," He repeated. This was not a Kodak moment! This was agony. (There's that word again.)

It might help for you to know a bit of my background. I was born an illegitimate child, and raised by a single mother who loved me deeply. Having survived a parade of six abusive stepfathers, I grew up believing pain and abandonment was "normal life." Looking back, I can understand why my mother turned to alcohol for relief. I saw the gut-wrenching heartache she suffered when she and I were mistreated.

Without even realizing it, I carried that pain with me into adulthood. I would have given anything to hear a father say, "Well done son. I'm so proud of you." But I never did.

During that otherwise typical day at the office, the Holy Spirit led me to plunge into a deep, dark corner of my heart, long frozen in time. I didn't know He was about to usher me into a new level of freedom that I had not experienced before. Standing in the middle of my office, I steadied myself on the back of a chair, and said, "Dad, thanks for life. I never met you, and that grieves me. I think you would be proud of me. Hopefully I will meet you on the other side."

That's all I could say. As soon as those words left my mouth, floodgates in my heart flew wide open. Emotion erupted from deep within and poured out of me in long, hard sobs. Wave after wave of pent-up grief was purged from my soul as rivers of living water washed away my pain (John 7:38).

Isn't it crazy the things that flash through your mind in a moment of crisis? One hundred and thirty feet below, in the dark hull of a ship, the Holy Spirit reminded me of that encounter with God. I began to see why I had been so driven, and why I had repeatedly risked my life for ridiculous things like seeing the interior of an old warship. It all boiled down to wanting the love and approval of a father I never had.

This isn't psychobabble. This is Holy Spirit revealed truth, and it's precisely why the Holy Spirit lead me to thank the father who abandoned me, for the one gift he gave me—life.

Back in Chuuk Lagoon, I wondered if I'd ever be able to break free. But what God did for me in those next moments is a picture of my life. In spite of zero visibility, the diver guide found me. Quick to assess the situation, he reached around behind me, unhooked my gear, and led me out of the dark. I was going to live! I could have kissed the guy, but refrained from such emotional expression in order to save air.

I had ample time to replay the events of the hour while I decompressed and slowly made my way back to the boat. Clinging to the anchor line, swaying back and forth in the ocean current,

I held my own private worship service while waiting for my computer to tell me it was safe to surface. I thanked God for my young guide and was reminded of a critical truth: breaking free from our hang-ups is never a solo experience. We need the Spirit of God and other fellow travelers to lead us to freedom.

The names and faces of people back home also passed through my mind. I thanked God for sending them my way, to help me break free from things that could have killed me. Things like alcohol, pornography, rage, and others.

Through the years my wife, Diane, has repeatedly reached into my heart, releasing me with her love. Godly men like Pastor Jack Hayford, Roy Hicks Jr., Butch, and many others have been spiritual dads to me. Their words of affirmation and encouragement have helped me see things in myself that I had never seen before. I'm so thankful for the East Hill Church family. It has been the extended family I never had growing up. In the midst of this loving circle of brothers and sisters, God's grace and truth continues to heal me.

Uncharted Waters

The Holy Spirit loves you too much to leave you the way you are. So count on this: When you pursue intimacy with God, the Holy Spirit will lead you into uncharted waters. He will prompt you to explore deep, dark places in your heart, particularly those areas where you feel trapped.

Why? Because He wants to liberate you. He wants to restore what sin has stolen, and usher you into the abundant life He planned for you from the very beginning.

One word of caution: never dive alone! Be sure to invite some safe friends on your journey. They'll see things you can't, and ways of escape you don't. They can help remove the hooks that are too hard for you to get to on your own. Peace and healing come in the context of relationships, not in isolation. God releases His transforming power when we connect with Him and with others.

God has ways of working that tend to fall outside the norm, and He's looking for people who will follow His lead and trust Him enough to go the distance. Are you game? Will you take the plunge of bold surrender, giving the Holy Spirit access to the deeper struggles of your heart? I can promise you this: Wherever He goes, liberty prevails. "Where the Spirit of the Lord is, there is freedom" (2 Cor. 3:17).

He's most eager to show you how wide, and how long, how deep, and how high His love really is for you. He bids you to come.

Precious Father, You and I both know my struggles. I get all tangled up in problems that overwhelm me. When I am tired and frustrated, I can easily forget that You are doing a good work in my life. The transforming work You began, You will complete. Lord, help me remember You are more concerned about my character than my comfort. I surrender the deepest struggles of my heart to You, and ask You to lead me into freedom. Show me the way. Bring people into my life who will help me in the journey. I trust You to turn my hang-ups into trophies of Your grace. Thanks, God. Amen.

CHAPTER 5

THE ONE WHO TRANSFORMS

Ted Roberts

*I*HATE SNAKES. WHEN I was a child, I lived in rattlesnake country and had a few close calls with the wily vermin. They scared me silly. Whenever one of those ugly things slithered into sight I bolted like a jackrabbit.

I'll never forget the time I found myself up-close-and-personal with a large cobra during jungle survival training in the Philippines. My native jungle guide remained completely undaunted as the two of us peered into the steely stare of that snake's eyes. He was used to these repulsive reptiles, but I wasn't. That wicked thing about stopped my heart.

King cobras are the King Kongs of the reptile world. The world's largest poisonous snake, they are also considered the most intelligent of all snakes. Gary Richard knows these serpents well, and has worked with them for years at the San Diego Zoo. For some reason I like the fact he hates cobras, too! He writes:

Don't you just hate King Cobras? I know I do, and I came to my feelings honestly. Our zoo had a thirteen foot giant Cobra, which seemed to be the embodiment of evil. He had a scar over his left eye that made him look even meaner, but more significantly, it kept him from shedding his skin in a normal fashion.

At least twice a year we got the dreaded call. The cobra had shed his skin but the eye cap didn't come off, so it had to be surgically removed. Special arrangements were critical because this snake is one of the most deadly. Its venom glands contain enough poison to kill one thousand adults—a fact that seemed to come up every time we did this procedure.

The curator of reptiles was assigned the task of grabbing the snake's head. Two other helpers steadied its body. Once the snake was subdued the vet began the delicate operation. My job was to assist the veterinarian.

The capture of the cobra was as follows. The five of us took our positions. Two helpers were on either side of the cage door. The curator was in front of the door. The vet and I were on either side of the curator. Sheer bird nets on the end of two-foot handles were our only defense. Seconds after the cage door was opened the King cobra appeared. When he saw us, he spread his cape and rose to his full stature. Our eyes fixated on this beast as it trembled with excitement and turned to select his prey. Lunging through the air towards the curator, it hissed and growled in malevolent rage.

The skilled assistants draped the netting over the snake's head. As it tried to force it's way through, the curator firmly grasped its neck just behind the venom sacks and the other assistants seized its writhing body. The Vet's hands trembled and beads of sweat ran down his forehead. The curator turned to me and said, "Quick! Get some paper towels!" in a strained voice, "Put them in the cobra's mouth." The cobra watched the paper towels as they were carefully positioned to allow him to bite them. He clamped down violently and began to chew the towels as they dripped with yellow venom.

In the middle of this torturous stress the curator spouts off, "Did you know that several elephants die every year from King Cobra bites? A man could never survive a bite with a full load of venom. That's why I had you drain its venom sacks." His closing comments left me shaking in my boots: "My hands are sweaty and my fingers are cramping. When I let go it may not be quick enough. More people are bitten trying to let go of snakes then when they grab them.[1]

One of my missions in life is to help folks who have foolishly or innocently grabbed hold of poisonous snakes—not the literal kind that crawl out from under rocks or slither through the woods. I'm talking figuratively about the kind of snakes that sneak in, craftily wrap around your soul, and slowly strangle the life out of you. Snakes like fear, anger, bitterness, alcohol, drugs, pornography, sexual bondage, and love addiction.

These are venomous snakes that strike at the heart and soul and can kill you. We live in an era when men and women desperately need the person of the Holy Spirit to help them drain the poison out of their lives and lead them to wholeness. In the last chapter I mentioned that long-lasting transformation is a "3-D" process. It involves the conscious mind, the unconscious mind, and the spiritual dimensions of your life.

On the conscious level you make the choice to deal with your hang-ups. With ruthless honesty and God's tender grace, you acknowledge your issues and bring them into the light of God's healing presence. You examine your thoughts and actions, and consistently bring them into alignment with God's truth (2 Cor. 10:5). But what about the deeper wounds of your soul? What about those intensely painful emotional memories stored outside your conscious awareness—the ones that jump-start you into fight or flight mode when triggered?

Two Divine Intercessors

During a combat tour of duty, I said yes to Jesus, and opened my heart to Him as my Savior. But the war left me with some brutal emotional scars. I had witnessed horrific events, embedding my memory with dreadful, graphic images.

After returning to the United States I couldn't sleep at night. Wicked flashbacks of violent war encounters intruded without warning. Over and over again the video replays appeared in my dreams, triggering agonizing memories of Vietnam. In utter desperation I cried out to God, pleading with Him to heal and deliver me from this torment.

Sometimes life is so painful and pressures so unbearable that we don't even know how to pray. I certainly didn't know how to pray about this problem in my life. But do you know that you have two divine intercessors who boldly persevere in believing prayer for you? It's true. Christ intercedes for you in heaven, and the Holy Spirit intercedes within you on earth (Rom. 8:34).

The apostle Paul tells us:

> The Spirit helps us in our weakness. We do not know what we ought to pray for, but the Spirit himself intercedes for us with groans that words cannot express. And he who searches our hearts knows the mind of the Spirit, because the Spirit intercedes for the saints in accordance with God's will.
>
> —ROMANS 8:26

In the midst of our sufferings, when we find ourselves consumed with anguish and overwhelmed by the enormity of our weaknesses, the Holy Spirit actively appeals to God for us. When we run out of resources, the Spirit takes over. When the inner groanings of our heart are too deep for words, He comes to our aid and communicates for us one on one, Spirit to Father. His petitions are always in keeping with God's will, and never muddied by our own personal agenda.

This is one of the most deeply personal activities of the Holy Spirit.[2] When you grieve, the Spirit grieves. When you hurt, He hurts. Your heartache breaks His heart. He sighs, groans, and understands your suffering, appealing to God on your behalf as your partner in healing.

The Holy Spirit knows us better than we know ourselves, and delights in pointing out the root issues that need the touch of God. Traumas and wounds that we have not exposed to God's healing power will drag us down, and keep us looking down at our shoelaces rather than up at heaven. When we are frustrated by ongoing issues, one of the best things we can do is ask God to show us what lies at the root of these problems, and how we need to pray. This isn't something we have to strive to do for ourselves. This is something we invite and allow the Spirit of God to accomplish for us.

In the last chapter I told you how the Holy Spirit stopped me one morning in the middle of my Bible study and said: "I want you to thank Me for your father." With pinpoint accuracy, He showed me the root of my emotional pain.

Children internalize the loss of a parent as a personal rejection. By obeying the Spirit's prompting, I opened the way for Him to enter into my conscious and unconscious grief memories, and all the ways that I had responded to the grief over being rejected. When I crossed over that invisible but very real barrier and thanked God for my father, waves of repressed pain came up and out. For years my mind had worked overtime to split-off these feelings from my awareness. But my heart remembered. As tears fell, the Holy Spirit moved mightily within me, healing the pain of my deprivation and loss.

As long as we hide, repress, or mask our emotional pain, it will continue to drive unhealthy behaviors. Repressed emotional pain shapes our life and robs us of freedom. Healing requires feeling. Embracing pain is a vital part of transformation. The addictions that afflicted me during young adulthood were merely misguided attempts to numb early psychological injuries and the traumatic sense of rejection I suffered from my birth father's abandonment (as well as from the six step-fathers who also walked out of my life).

Through that one step of obedience the Holy Spirit released me from emotional bonds that I had not previously recognized. His work in the deep places of my soul that afternoon was nothing short of supernatural.

A Deeper Level of Healing

There are some problems in life that we simply cannot solve on our own. They require a deeper level of healing by the Spirit of God. The Holy Spirit wants to heal the places in your heart that store your emotional memories and pain. He wants to soothe and clean old wounds, and set you free to move forward in God's plans and purposes for your life.

When I was healing from Post Traumatic Stress[3] after the war, the Lord challenged me to pray in the Spirit each night before I went to sleep (Eph. 6:18). The biblical Greek word *en pneumatic* "in the Spirit" literally means, "in the spiritual realm and with the Holy Spirit's aid."[4]

I'll have to admit I really didn't understand why He asked me to do this, but I knew very clearly that He was prompting me this direction each night when my head hit the pillow. My wife is my witness. Within a few months the night terrors and flashbacks stopped. I have not had any since.

Why did God ask me to pray in the Spirit before I went to sleep? I think I understand the reasons better now than I did then. Recent research on the brain tells us that whatever you read, see, listen to, hear, or experience during the last forty-five minutes of the day has a profound effect on your sleep and the following day. During sleep your unconscious mind replays and processes this late-night input up to six times more frequently than anything else you experience during your waking hours. If you spend the last part of your day communing with God, these interactions will be replayed in your mind through the night. This opens the door for the Spirit of God to heal and speak to your unconscious mind during your sleep.

David, who had experienced more than his share of life trauma, took note of this nighttime healing ministry in his several of his psalms. He wrote:

> I will praise the LORD, who counsels me; even at night my heart instructs me.
> —PSALM 16:7

Later, another psalmist exulted over a similar thought:

> By day the LORD directs his love, at night his song is with me—a prayer to the God of my life.
> —PSALM 42:8

Healing occurs when our spirits are united with the Spirit of God. I don't really know where the conscious mind ends and the unconscious mind begins. It's a bit of a mystery. But I do know the Holy Spirit lives in me, and that my spirit is one with His. The place where Christ lives in me is whole, and He will continue to bring the wounded places in my soul into His healing light.

Running New Software

We all know that the brain is an amazing computer. In simple terms, it consists of two main parts: the neocortex and the limbic system. The neocortex in the front of your brain is the location of your higher level thinking functions. It is your supervisor that helps you make plans, control impulses, make good (or bad) decisions, and stay focused. It receives, organizes, and stores information for recall.[5]

The limbic system lies near the center of your brain. Though not much bigger than a walnut, it is power-packed with functions that affect your behavior and survival. This is the portion of the brain that stores highly charged emotional memories, sets the emotional tone of the mind, emotionally colors external events, and tags certain things as important.

If you have been traumatized by a dramatic event, such as being in an accident, or being abandoned, betrayed, or abused by a parent or spouse, the emotional component of the memory is stored in the limbic system of the brain.

This is also the component of your mind that controls all the automatic systems of the body, such as our fight or flight survival responses. Now there is a key difference between the front of our brain and this little walnut shaped center in our brain. The limbic system doesn't have an organized memory like the neocortex and therefore can't tell the difference between yesterday and 20 years ago.[6] This is why the recall of a years-ago childhood trauma can trigger powerful emotions in us today.

Drugs, alcohol, and other compulsive behaviors can program the limbic system to avoid the awareness of uncomfortable thoughts and feelings, instead of making healthy responses to resolve the fear.[7] This helps us understand why an alcoholic or a person in sexual bondage can deeply believe in Christ, and yet act in ways that totally discredit his or her faith.

I grew up in a very violent home. When I expressed weakness around my stepfather, he hit me for being a wimp. I learned very quickly to not need *anything*, and to keep quiet about what I felt. In order to survive in this environment, I withdrew and "toughened up." All through my childhood, these were the game rules.

My limbic system logged the emotional memories well. Now, jump ahead twenty years. I am married to my wife, Diane, and I hear her say, "Come on honey, talk to me. Why do you withdraw when you get upset?"

I remember those words as if they happened yesterday because they triggered such intense emotion. My limbic system's bells and whistles sounded off. Danger sirens screamed: "Don't open up! You'll get killed!" It was so confusing because my neocortex knew that I deeply loved Diane, and wanted to be open with her. These automatic survival reactions could have easily destroyed our marriage and ruined our kids—except for the grace of God. *Thank heaven!*

The Holy Spirit is the Spirit of grace (Zech. 12:10; Heb. 10:29). The root *chanan* for grace, means "to act graciously or mercifully toward someone; to be compassionate and favorably inclined." In the Bible, the word *grace* is often woven into the context of a relationship with the Giver of grace. We should not use the word grace as if we were describing some kind of commodity that God dispenses—like unleaded gas from a pump. Instead, God comes to you in the Person of the Holy Spirit in ways that are kind, compassionate, and brimming over with His love. He is always rooting for you. He delights in you and unconditionally accepts you just the way you are. He desires to lead you with unfailing love, just as He led me to open up with my wife. His love has the ability to seep down into the fundamental core of who you are and make you whole.

Delight in the Spirit's Work Within You

As you deal with your hang-ups, delight in the Spirit's work within you. Do what He does: Give yourself grace, and be patient with yourself. Tell yourself the truth: "I may be confused and conflicted, but the Spirit of the living God lives in me and He is doing a powerful work. He is healing me. He is restoring me from the inside out. He will finish the work He started. God is alive in my spirit, and He is mending the fractures in my soul. What is impossible for me is possible with Him. I am born again of His Spirit and the Spirit of Him who raised Jesus from the dead is living in me. He is present with me right now, actively bringing life to my body, soul, and spirit. His life source flows within me, permeating my conscious and unconscious mind to conform me to the image of His Son.

Remember Jesus' promise?

> If anyone is thirsty, let him come to me and drink. Whoever believes in me, as the Scripture has said, streams of living water will flow from within him. By this he meant the Spirit, whom those who believed in Him were later to receive. Up to that time the Spirit had not been given, since Jesus had not yet been glorified.
>
> —JOHN 7:37–39

I wish I could say that transformation happens fast. More often than not, it doesn't. That doesn't mean God is out of the miracle business. Not even close! But what I typically see—and what I have experienced in my own life—is His supernatural work coupled with my human process. For instance, the Spirit's revelation to me about my need to thank God for my father was supernatural. It was my responsibility to obey Him, and embrace my grief. *Feeling* lead to *healing*.

Most emotional wounds are not healed with one single prayer. God will not remove your brain, with its memory banks, and shove in a new one. Typically He doesn't rewire your limbic system. Instead, the Spirit of God offers to fellowship with you and lead you into freedom. He speaks words of comfort to your heart: *I know about your secret pain. I grieve with you. I'm here to help you bear the burden of your suffering. I will lead you into truth. I will show you the way to health and wholeness. Don't run from your heartache. Embrace it.*

> Come to me. Get away with me and you'll recover your life. I'll show you how to take a real rest. Walk with me and work with me—watch how I do it. Learn the unforced

rhythms of grace. I won't lay anything heavy or ill-fitting on you. Keep company with me and you'll learn to live freely and lightly.

— MATTHEW 11:28–30, THE MESSAGE

The Spirit who resides within you is keenly aware of your frailties. He knows when you are wrestling with a "limbic lag." This is the time gap between what the organizational front of your brain grasps and what your limbic system experiences. This is precisely why living out our faith can be such a struggle for us. Besides the fact that we are born with a bent to sin, this also plays a part in why we do what we don't want to do, and don't do what we want to do, as Paul agonized over in Romans 7.

One Decision at a Time

Deep transformation occurs one decision at a time. No matter what your emotions tell you, do what is right. Do the right thing and God will bless you. Transformation requires doing the right thing no matter how you feel. And the right thing is usually the hard thing.

It took me years to break the automatic response of withdrawing from my wife when I felt insecure or threatened. For years, my emotions screamed: *Being open will get you killed!* But every time I pushed through and got to the other side of doing what I knew was right, I'd sense the Spirit say, "See that wasn't too bad was it? You didn't die. In fact you feel better after a good heart to heart talk, don't you?"

Abandon your searches for quick cures. Be patient with yourself and the Holy Spirit. Patience does not mean passivity. As Dr. Jack Hayford puts it, it is a proactive choice to exercise restraint. As you commune with God, trust the Spirit to show you what you need to see, when you need to see it. Trust Him with the timing of your healing. He really does know more than you know, and

He is *always* working within you for your highest good.

I had to learn to be patient with myself and to stop beating myself up, like my stepfathers did, when I didn't respond in right ways. The transformation process began picking up speed once I started to give myself grace.

When the Holy Spirit comes to dwell within you, you no longer have to settle for living according to your past programming. You no longer have to be dominated and controlled by the automatic responses of your limbic system. The Holy Spirit removes the label of victim from you, and declares that you are more than conquerors in Christ. He will lead you into victory over pre-programmed impulses.

As I said earlier, the process is usually gradual, extending over time. Some transformation requires agonizing times of grief when we connect the facts of our wounds with feelings, and work through the pain that we've repressed. The greater the loss, the greater the pain, the greater the healing.

If you were led to expect some genie-out-of-the-bottle instant transformation when you became a believer, you were bound to be disappointed. Being transformed into the character of Christ involves struggle. No one else can get rid of your inner conflicts for you. No one else can pray a magical prayer that suddenly erases your distorted thinking or painful memories. *You must work with the Holy Spirit.* His transformation requires your cooperation. He will provide the energy you need to endure the task.

> Be energetic in your life of salvation, reverent and sensitive before God. That energy is God's energy, an energy deep within you, God himself willing and working at what will give him the most pleasure.
> —PHILIPPIANS 2:12–13, THE MESSAGE

So how can we collaborate with the Holy Spirit? We bring our wrong attitudes to Him, confess our faults, and allow Him to cleanse our hearts. We bring our twisted thinking and negativity to Him and ask Him to show us how to think straight by speaking to us through the Scriptures.

We invite Him to expose the lies we have believed and to redirect us to truth. We invite His perspectives. We ask Him to reveal Himself, and to show us images and words that will help us understand what He is doing in us in the moment. We memorize and pray through Scripture so that it will seep down into the deepest recesses of our soul, and leave a permanent imprint on our reasoning processes. We choose to patiently endure the change process and delight in God's promise to finish what He started in us at salvation (Phil. 1:6).

Make no mistake, my friend. When you're wrestling with snakes from hell you're going to need patience—divine patience. Deep, long-lasting transformation is characterized by Holy Spirit empowered patience—a fruit he enjoys growing and displaying in our lives.

+ Delight in the fruit of the Spirit within you.

+ Delight in His ability to help you restrain the angry words you want to spew at yourself or others.

+ Delight in the courage He gives you to open up when you want to shut down.

+ Delight in His ability to reveal the source of the pain that drives your compulsions.

+ Delight in His kindness to expose the lies you've believed, and to lead you into freedom.

+ Delight in His ability to heal the traumas you can't even remember.

- Delight in the energy and perseverance He provides to endure grueling seasons of chronic stress.

- Delight in the patience He gives you for others, who like you, are also wrestling with snakes. All of us fight the snake of sin and have done things we're not proud of.

- *Be delighted!* His incomparably great power is consistently working in you, dramatically transforming you in ways that will leave His imprint on your generation.

Decide to Be a Generation Changer

Transformation is a 3-D process. First we break *denial*, face reality and deal with our hang-ups. Next we purposely *delight* in the Spirit's work within us. And finally we *decide* to be generation changers who leave a godly legacy for those who follow.

It amazes me that I can read a book in the Bible numerous times, and totally miss a truth that had been staring me in the face for years. When I first came to the Lord, the Book of Revelation captivated me. I was trained to fly nuclear delivery missions and had experienced war up close and personal. It's clear to me that this world is headed for a showdown. At some point the wounded heart of mankind will pull the trigger.

Charts and graphs about the end times, based on the Book of Revelation fascinate me. But these foldout schematics are simply man's best guess about how things could play out. God's orchestration of His plans will likely far exceed our comprehension. What truly stuns me is that God has invited us to partner with Him in accomplishing His plans and purposes—even as He scripts the coming chapters of human history.

If you read Revelation from start to finish, you'll discover twenty different choruses of worship lifted to the Lord.[8] Each chorus is directly tied to the purposes and actions of God. The choruses repeatedly declare that it is God's presence—His Person and His power moving into a situation—that transforms it and devastates the plans of hell.

Through worship, we have the privilege of entering into partnership with God, and co-labor with Him in the fulfillment of His plans. Worship is the stage upon which God steps forth in His sovereign power to bring about His purposes. It's not that our worship provokes a sovereign God to act. Rather it is His abiding Spirit within us that provokes us to worship. And when we worship, things are changed in the spirit realm that impact our present and future generations.

Bless the Lord at All Times

King David, one of the world's most renowned worship leaders, wrote nearly half of the Book of Psalms. It is one of the most intimate and relational books of the Bible, and reveals David's deep heart connection with God. In his writings, worship and praise are revealed as the means by which God's rule is invited into our dire circumstances. David declares: "You are holy, Enthroned in the praises of Israel" (Ps. 22:3, NKJV).

One of the most remarkable and exciting things about honest and sincere worship is that it opens the way for God's effective and overruling entry into our confusion and chaos. When we worship God in the face of perplexing circumstances and unruly situations, we invite God to establish His rule amid our turmoil. We open the door for the divine order already secured in heaven (Ps. 119:89, NKJV) to be realized here and now in our lives.

Although God is present everywhere, a distinct manifestation of His rule is established in the environment of praise. He inhabits (*yawshab*, "to remain, to settle, or marry") our praise. God's ruling presence abides with us when we worship, and brings order to that which is out of order.[9]

Throughout the centuries David's songs and poems have been a source of personal inspiration and strength. His emotionally drenched complaints, humble confessions, desperate pleas, penitent prayers, and jubilant songs of praise have helped many express the yearnings of their heart.

David's commitment to worship without ceasing speaks volumes about the extraordinary depth of his relationship with God. His unrelenting determination to *bless the Lord at all times*, even in the most discouraging circumstances, dramatically influenced others towards a lifestyle of worship.

Through the ages, genuine worship has been the common denominator among the supernatural visitations of God. The one thing that has characterized every transformation of a people and a culture is that clouds of praise preceded the rain of Christ's blessing and the release of His power.

Of all his accomplishments, what was David's highest achievement in this world? We find the capstone of David's life mentioned in the Book of Acts:

> For when David had served God's purpose in his own generation, he fell asleep; he was buried with his fathers.
>
> —ACTS 13:36

God highlights the fact that David served His purpose in his own generation. This worshiper was a generation changer. The blessings of God we enjoy today are linked with David's choice to worship and fully trust God's promise to him. He served God in such a way that it shaped his generation and ours.

In the closing chapter of the Bible, David receives another honorable mention: "I, Jesus, have sent My angel to testify to you these things in the churches. I am the Root and the Offspring of David, the Bright and Morning Star" (Rev. 22:16, NKJV).

Now maybe you are thinking, "Hey, wait a minute. David wasn't all that great. He made some lousy choices that destroyed people's lives and hurt his family and friends." Yes, that's true. And so did Abraham, Jacob, Moses, Sarah, Gideon, Jepthah, and a host of others who loved God. Most of those mentioned in Hebrews 11, The Hall of Fame for Heroes of Faith, failed at some point in their lives. But each individual listed in Hebrews 11 was also a generation changer.

This milestone New Testament chapter reviews the triumphant experiences of numerous heroes of faith. We find a description of how faith works. Faith is an established conviction concerning things unseen and a settled expectation of future reward. God commended these men and women, but not because of their achievements, personal holiness, or passive acceptance of divine promises. He gave them a good report *because of their faith*—their active certitude expressed in obedience, persistence, and sacrifice.

The Divine Arranger

The writer of Hebrews makes a statement at the beginning of that eleventh chapter that has puzzled me for years. Somehow, it seemed out of place to me:

> By faith we understand that the worlds were framed by the word of God, so that the things which are seen were not made of things which are visible.
> —HEBREWS 11:3, NKJV

At first glance the verse seems like an odd tangent. Why would the writer suddenly veer off the topic of individual heroes, shift his focus to the creation of the world, and then return to highlight faithful saints of old?

After digging deeper I discovered there is more to this verse than meets the eye. The Greek word used for "worlds" is not *cosmos*, which refers to the universe. Nor is it *ghay*, which refers to the earth. The word is *ahee-ohn*, which speaks of a specific period of time, an age, or a generation.[10] The author is essentially saying, "Through faith we understand that different times periods, ages, and generations in human history were framed by the Word of God."

Notice the writer said *framed* by the Word of God, not "created" by the Word of God. The word choice was divinely inspired. The Greek word translated "framed," *katartizo*, is rich with meaning. It means to arrange, to set in order, equip, complete what is lacking, to make fully ready, repair, and prepare. It is the same word used for the disciples mending their nets, and for restoring a fallen brother.

The writer of Hebrews is saying, "Through faith we understand that various generations were set in order, repaired, and restored by the Word of God." The rest of the chapter lists individuals who reshaped their generation as they lived in deep communion with God and according to His divine principles. They are men and women who purposefully pursued intimacy with God and allowed His Word to shape their thoughts and actions. They believed what God said to them and acted in line with His Word. And the result? Like David, their faith had a visible revolutionary impact on their personal human experience, on the time period in which they lived, and on generations to come.

Let's be honest. We all have hang-ups. It's impossible to live in this bruised and broken world without being wounded. No one escapes unscathed. All of us have said and done things that have hurt those nearest and dearest to us. But that doesn't have to be the end of the story!

We can decide to be a generation changer. We can choose to deal with our hang-ups and not pass them on to our children and grandchildren. *The dysfunctional family patterns we grew up with can stop with us.*

It doesn't matter how destructive our backgrounds were. It doesn't matter how much reprogramming our distorted thought patterns or traumatized limbic systems need. As we go deeper with God He will show us how to cooperate with Him in the transformation process. His Spirit will empower us, one choice at a time, to do what is right regardless of what our emotions say.

As we delight in the Spirit's work within us and lift our hearts in worship, God will establish His divine order in all that concerns us. It will happen moment by moment, day by day, week by week, and year after year.

Isn't it great to know that—in the big scheme of things—we're on the winning side? Mark Twain once wryly observed: "I admire the serene assurance of those who have faith. It is wonderful to observe the calm confidence of a Christian with four aces."[11] His words put a smile on my face—and ring a hallelujah in my soul.

It boils down to this. You and I are in the middle of a rigged game. The cards are stacked. We are holding all the aces. In Christ we can't fail. The conclusion has already been published. Those who are born of the Spirit get the reward (John 3:5–8; Rev. 22:12).

And what's the reward? His name is Jesus.

> *Come, Holy Spirit, and deeply transform me. Heal my emotional memories so that I won't overreact to people and situations as I have in the past. I welcome You to renew my conscious and unconscious mind. Reveal my twisted ways of thinking in the light of Your truth. Grant me the strength to make decisions based on what is right and true, rather than on my emotions. Thank You for being so gracious and patient with me. Help me to be patient with myself as You transform me, one day at a time, into a generation changer.*

Chapter 6
The One Who Unites

Pam Vredevelt

*M*RS. VREDEVELT, I believe your baby has Down syndrome. He isn't breathing well and we are trying to help him with oxygen."

In disbelief my emotions began to run wild and unchecked. Engulfed in a jumble of scrambled thoughts I wanted desperately to hear the doctor say, "Wait a minute. I'm wrong. I've made a mistake. Your son is fine." Those words never came.

I wasn't tracking well and blurted out, "What does this mean?"

"It means your son will be mentally retarded. There is a catheter in his heart and the technicians are still working to stabilize him."

I spent that night alone in my hospital room listening to happy families around me celebrating their babies. My own personal doctor was in Russia. My pediatrician was on vacation. My parents were in California. John was with our other children at home, and a tiny little boy named Nathan Vredevelt was in some sterile room under impersonal fluorescent lights, fighting for his life.

And me? I never felt more alone and confused in all my life. As hot tears rolled down my cheeks, I remember whispering into the night, "Why did my body betray me? Oh God, how could You have let this happen to my little boy?"

I wrestled with the *whys* for a long time after Nathan was born. Shortly after we came home from the hospital with Nathan, Kay, a precious lady from our church, called. "I'm coming over to clean your house," she said. "What's a good day?"

She showed up on my doorstep a couple days later with our friend Delight. What a sight greeted my eyes when I opened the front door. These two looked like they'd just stepped off the set of a sci-fi movie—with buckets on their heads, gas masks on their faces, combat boots, striped socks, and aprons to cover outfits that would have been rejected by the homeless.

They came to make me laugh. It worked! But Kay and Delight's visit was far more significant to me than the laughter—or the clean floors and dusted furniture they left behind. Kay is the mother of two, Kurt and Kara. We'd known the family over many years because their son was in our youth group years ago when John and I worked with teens. Kara, their youngest, was born with cerebral palsy, and over the years had gone through extensive surgeries. For twelve years Kay had walked the path I was just beginning.

When I saw her standing there in that crazy getup on my porch, smiling from ear to ear, I remembered the many times I'd seen her in the past and thought, *She has such burdens; how can she be so happy?*

I plopped myself in our big stuffed chair in the living room to nurse Nathan and said, "Kay, I'm struggling with something. I don't know how to view Nathan's Down syndrome from God's perspective. How do you see it?"

The wise lady that she is, Kay didn't give me any simple platitudes or pat answers. Instead, she pointed me back to Scripture. One of the passages that had been meaningful to them since

Kara's birth, she told me, was John chapter 9. I had my copy of The Message at hand. Eager for answers I picked it up and began to read:

> Walking down the street, Jesus saw a man blind from birth. His disciples asked, "Rabbi, who sinned: this man or his parents, causing him to be born blind?" Jesus said, "You're asking the wrong question. You're looking for someone to blame. There is no such cause-effect here. Look instead for what God can do."
>
> —JOHN 9:1–3, THE MESSAGE

Look instead for what God can do.* Kay's visit was key in my healing. As she shared what God had taught her from the Bible, the Lord spoke to me. He challenged me to shift my focus, to quit trying to "figure it all out," and to believe that He had eternally significant purposes for our little boy. I was to look for what God was doing in the midst of all that we were going through.

Change Agents

People like Kay, who are intentional about loving God and loving others, are change agents. After you spend time with them, you're different. No, everything isn't perfect, but it's *better*. Noticeably better. We all need at least a couple of these safe traveling companions as we journey through life.

One of the first things Jesus did in His public ministry was to gather a small group of companions. After an all night prayer vigil alone on a mountain, He called His followers together and chose twelve guys who became His band of brothers (Luke 6:12–16).

There was nothing tentative about Christ's call to community. He didn't timidly inch His way into conversations and say, "Hey

---

* Excerpted from *The Power of Letting Go* © 2006 by Pam Vredevelt. Used by permission of Multnomah Publishers, Inc.

everyone, I'm thinking about forming a group. I'd kind of like you to think about joining it. I know you're really busy. I know you're working a couple of jobs to make ends meet, and you've got kids, and a lot of other things going on. But I'd really like you to be a part of my group.

"Oh, but I need to warn you…sometimes My people do dumb things. They'll let you down. Others will confuse you. You won't understand them because they're wired completely different. Some may even drive you crazy. But, hey, just think about it and get back to Me when it's convenient."

One of my favorite Catholic authors, Henry Nouwen, said it well: "Community is the place where the person you least want to be with is always there." The original twelve probably experienced this right along with the rest of us. Can you imagine the sparks that flew when Simon and Matthew had to share a tent together? By societal standards, these men were archenemies.

Simon was a zealot. He belonged to a gang of fanatic Jewish extremists who violently resisted Roman influence. Matthew worked for the Roman government as a tax gatherer. This shrewd shark of a man lay awake at night plotting ways to siphon the common folk's wages. I have a hunch these two guys duked-it-out more than once.

But their differences didn't bother Jesus. He was deliberate and intentional about choosing each one of them. Diversity catalyzes growth and change far more effectively than uniformity.

The religious leaders of the day, however, were deeply invested in uniformity. When Jesus welcomed Matthew into His inner circle, evidently others of the outcast classes followed closely behind. And the religious leaders had a fit.

> When Jesus was eating supper at Matthew's house with his close followers, a lot of disreputable characters came and joined them. When the Pharisees saw him [Jesus] keeping this kind of company, they had a fit, and lit into Jesus' followers. "What kind of example is this from your Teacher, acting cozy with crooks and riffraff?" Jesus, overhearing, shot back,

"Who needs a doctor: the healthy or the sick? Go figure out
what this Scripture means: 'I'm after mercy, not religion.' I'm
here to invite outsiders, not coddle insiders."
—MATTHEW 9:10–13. THE MESSAGE

The same tensions exist today.

* Jesus is inclusive. Pharisees are exclusive.

* Jesus opens His arms. Pharisees turn their backs.

* Jesus calls for unity. Pharisees demand uniformity.

* Jesus forgives. Pharisees forbid.

* Jesus develops. Pharisees devalue.

* Jesus looks at people and smiles. Pharisees roll
  their eyes and smirk.

To those who have been told by the Pharisees of this world,
"You're not good enough," Jesus says, "I choose you."

I've played the Pharisee more times than I care to admit—in my
marriage, with my kids, and with fellow believers in the church. Oh,
I had my rational arguments and they had theirs. But I really didn't
want to hear their side of the story. At the time I was convinced they
had made the bigger errors. They were more at fault than me. The
Pharisee within me stood tall, not wanting to budge an inch.

And the results were alienation, self-deception, and grief to
the Spirit of God. God is love and anything that isn't love pains
Him. I recall getting word that a church in another city had hired
a person who had deeply wounded me years ago. The announce-
ment stunned me—and then tied my stomach in knots. I was
so angry. Everything in me wanted to catch a plane and make
an appointment to fill the church leaders in on "all the details."
Surely they deserved to know the truth. At the very least, wasn't
a letter to those in charge my civic duty?

As I contemplated how I would speak the truth (plot my

revenge), a clear corrective word rang through the corridors of my mind: *The government shall be upon My shoulders, Pam, not yours.* Ouch. I recognized the voice of the Spirit and wept over my truculent pride. Incidentally, this event occurred a few years ago, and God is doing a phenomenal work in and through that individual.

There's a bit of Pharisee in all of us that boldly says: I want what I want, when I want it. This anti-God attitude eats away at our relationships like a fast-growing cancer. Jesus warns us to steer clear of it.

> If you walk around with your nose in the air, you're going to end up flat on your face, but if you're content to be simply yourself, you will become more than yourself.
> —LUKE 18:14, THE MESSAGE

Radical Commitment to Relationship

You know what astonished people about Jesus? You know what caused people to leave everything and follow Him? They felt His passionate love for them—something they had never experienced in the presence of other religious leaders. When He looked into their eyes and said, "I choose you," His love penetrated their souls. The purity of His devotion was 100 percent genuine and convincing. When people saw their reflection in His grace-filled eyes they knew, through and through, that He believed in them. He liked them. He valued them. They felt increasingly significant whenever they were with Him. Their worth was never in question.

That's why these believers endured beatings, imprisonment, torture, and cruel deaths in their later years. They were willing to die for Jesus because He, and the love they shared in community, had radically transformed their lives.

Jesus didn't tell His followers, "If you prefer, you can just read The Book, listen to My lectures, and use the independent study method." He never said or modeled anything remotely close to this. He did just the opposite. He taught and lived a radical commitment to a relationship with God and with others. Both connections are vitally intertwined.

Remember what Jesus said to the religious expert who asked Him to define the greatest commandment? He said, "Love the Lord your God with all your heart and with all your soul and with all your mind. This is the first and greatest commandment." We often stop right there. But Jesus didn't. He went on: "And the second is like it: Love your neighbor as yourself. All the Law and the Prophets hang on these two commandments" (Matt. 22:37–40).

Every life, no matter how outwardly "together" it may appear, bears scars, often hidden, tucked away, out of public view. And these old wounds, only partially healed over, remind us of our need for God's love, and our need to be loved by others. It's true that our greatest wounds happen in relationships. Human nature, at its core, can be coldhearted and hotheaded.

My dad retired from his job as a vice president at Honeywell several years ago, having weathered many years of bloody corporate politics. For as long as I can remember, Dad has been a loving mentor and my chief confidante. Early on in my life he shared a slice of wisdom that I've never forgotten: "Pam, your toughest challenges in life won't be tasks, they'll be people." His words ring true both in the corporate world, and in the local church.

That's why we need a Savior. That's why Jesus left the comforts of heaven for you and for me. He came to reconcile humanity to God and to make peace possible in our relationships with one another. It is also why we need a fresh filling—daily, hourly, moment-by-moment—of the Holy Spirit. It is impossible to keep the spirit of unity in the bond of peace without His supernatural assistance (Eph. 4:3). We're simply too selfish.

Your deepest wounds happen in relationships, and so does your deepest healing. It's the way we're wired. God designed you to be a part of His family: "His unchanging plan has always been to adopt us into his own family by bringing us to himself through

Jesus Christ...this gave him great pleasure" (Eph. 1:5, NLT).

From the beginning of time, God chose to make a covenant, not with individuals, but with a people who would carry on His purposes. While we enter God's family individually through faith in Christ, the goal of salvation has always been the same: God is saving a people, a community of believers, who will bear His name and put His love on display (Exod. 19:5–6; 2 Cor. 6:16–18).

Your faith in God may be deeply personal, but He never intended for it to be private. You cannot experience the fullness of God's love flying solo. The depths of God are experienced in the context of His family.

God's Family, the Church

Another name for God's family is "the church of the living God." (See 1 Timothy 3:15, GWT.) The church is now the expression of Jesus on earth. The word for church, *ekklesia*, is an ancient Greek term for the people of a kingdom who are called to take their role as responsible citizens. Used ninety-two times in the New Testament, the word refers to a local church congregation.

God spotlights the elevated importance of the church: "The church, you see, is not peripheral to the world; the world is peripheral to the church. The church is Christ's body, in which he speaks and acts, by which he fills everything with his presence" (Eph. 1:23, THE MESSAGE).

If you're not a part of a local church, please, investigate the options in your area. Ask God to lead you to a church that will best meet your needs, and where you can serve others with your talents. Ask Him to guide you to a fellowship where the Word is taught, the love is evident, and the worship is passionate. God has gifted you in specific ways for specific assignments. He knows best where you will thrive in community. Avoid being a spectator who casually drops in on services now and then. Actively engage.

The times you least want to go to church are probably the

times when you most need to be there, soaking up the presence of God like a thirsty sponge. If you want to go deeper with God, you've got to carve out time with Him. Make it a habit to participate in a local church community so that you don't miss out on the spiritual blessings God has in store for you.

> Some people have gotten out of the habit of meeting for worship, but we must not do that. We should keep on encouraging each other, especially since you know that the day of the Lord's coming is getting closer.
> —HEBREWS 10:25, CEV

The credibility of Christ's entire mission rests on the choices we make in community with one another. When differences arise within the family of God (notice I said when, not if), we must remember that we are all on the same side. Christ already tore down the wall of hostility between us. Your God is my God. We have equal access to the Father (Eph. 2:14–16). The Spirit who lives in you also lives in me. We are members of one another (Rom. 12:5; Eph. 4:25). As Spirit people we are commissioned to:

+ Build up one another (1 Thess. 5:11).

+ Care for one another (1 Cor. 12:25).

+ Love one another (1 Thess. 3:12, 4:9).

+ Pursue one another's good (Rom. 14:19).

+ Bear with one another in love (Eph. 4:2).

+ Bear one another's burdens (Gal. 6:2).

+ Be kind and compassionate to one another (1 Thess. 5:15).

+ Forgive one another (Col. 3:13).

+ Submit to one another (Eph. 5:21).

+ Consider one another better than us (Phil. 2:3).

+ Be devoted to one another in love (Rom. 12:10).

+ Live in peace with one another (Rom. 12:18).

What would happen if all of us took these words seriously and acted on them? What if you and I gave 100 percent of our energies, and daily asked for a fresh filling of the Holy Spirit to aggressively follow these instructions? Can you imagine how fun and life-changing our church communities would be? Can you imagine the buzz that would hit the airwaves if people actually witnessed THAT kind of love in action? There is no advertising or public relations firm in the world that could come close to creating the resulting impact on the community. I know of what I speak. I have received that kind of love.

The Sunday Morning Brigade

After Nathan was born, I was unable to attend church because of his health complications and compromised immune system. He just wasn't strong enough to be around that many people.

It wasn't long, however, before some kind ladies in the church figured out I was absent, and called with an idea. Marylee said, "Pam, let's form a Sunday Morning Brigade. Give me the names of several ladies you'd like to come to your home to take care of Nathan so you can go to church. We'll each take one Sunday a month." And that's just what happened. For the next year and a half, Marylee, Kathy, Margaret, and Joy came one Sunday a month to be with Nathan while I attended services. Sugar and Lynn stepped in to help, too.

I can't tell you how much that two hours a week meant to me.* My life had been turned upside down by Nathan's diagnosis,

---

* Excerpted from *Angel Behind the Rocking Chair* © 1999 by Pam Vredevelt. Used by permission of Multnomah Publishers, Inc.

and I was having a very difficult time adjusting to all the implications. Being with God's family helped. I sat in the presence of God crying through worship as I let go of my grief.

The Holy Spirit helped me wrap words around my feelings and communicate my heart to God. I soaked in Pastor Ted's words of strength, comfort, and hope, experiencing first hand the power of God's healing presence in the midst of His church.

Through the years I've heard horrific accounts of churches that have blown apart at the seams. I'm sure you've heard the stories, too: "So and so did such and such, then this led to that—and the church fell apart."

What causes these catastrophes? What drives division and dissention? What energizes discord? What leads us to bite, devour, and destroy one another? (Gal. 5:15). I think it boils down to one dirty little four-letter word: self. Rifts and factions happen when we live life according to me, myself, and I rather than according to the Spirit.

Seventeen Ways to Break God's Heart

Do you want to know what brings tears to God's eyes? Do you want to know how to break His heart? Just in case you'd like to know, I've compiled an abridged list of offenses certain to accomplish such a goal.

+ Remove God from the center of your life and place your ego there instead.

+ Listen to the voice of the Pharisee rather than the voice of the Spirit.

+ Don't practice the presence of God; practice the presence of self.

+ Be acutely tuned in to your own needs, feelings, and desires.

+ Live as if life is all about you.

+ Be good to people as long as they serve your purposes and give you what you want.

+ When people inconvenience or frustrate you, be smart. Don't let it happen again.

+ Drive to dominate, possess, maneuver, and cover things over to get your way.

+ Seek to impress.

+ Keep score.

+ Stockpile offenses.

+ Demand your rights.

+ Protect your image.

+ Justify your actions.

+ Give yourself mercy and others judgment.

+ Don't let others put away their past. Remind them of their mistakes while dismissing your own.

+ And by all means, surround yourself with people who tell you what you want to hear rather than the truth.

Do these things overtly. Do them covertly. By doing so, I assure you, you will energize discord, break the bond of peace, and grieve the heart of God.

These kind of offenses insult the Spirit of grace (Heb. 10:29). Some theologians believe that insulting the Spirit of grace may be identified with blasphemy against the Spirit. Blasphemy against the Spirit is the continual and deliberate rejection of the Holy

Spirit's witness to Christ, to His Word, and to His convicting work against sin.[1]

There is a more excellent way. And Jesus leads us there.

Willing Sacrifice

Shortly before He left this world, the Savior prayed for you and me:

> My prayer is not for them alone. I pray also for those who will believe in me through their message, that all of them may be one, Father, just as you are in me and I am in you. May they also be in us so that the world may believe that you have sent Me. *I have given them the glory that you gave me, that they may be one as we are one: I in them and you in me.* May they be brought to *complete unity* to let the world know that you sent me and have loved them even as you have loved me."
>
> —JOHN 17:20–23, EMPHASIS ADDED

What is "the glory" Christ has given us so that we can "become one"? The glory of Christ was displayed on the cross. It was His self-denial and willingness to lay down His life in order to save the human race. In Christ's weakest hour He performed His most glorious work.

The cross is the ultimate picture of God's love. When Jesus hung and bled and died, God was saying to the world, "I love you." Before going to the cross, Jesus said, "Greater love has no one than this, that he lay down his life for his friends." To those who were willing to listen He said, "Take up your cross and follow Me" (Matt. 16:24).

But what does that really mean? What does this entail? It involves deliberate sacrifice, the crucifixion of our pride-filled ego, the setting aside of our personal desires for the sake of the common good, and the synchronization of our life with the rhythm of the Spirit where loss brings gain, death brings life, and humility brings honor. Someone said it well: "The cross is 'I' crossed out."

Let's be honest. Living in harmony with others is easier said than done. Unconditional love demands supernatural empowerment. Just look at the disciples. Before they were filled with the Holy Spirit they jockeyed for position, strove to be top dog, bickered, sniped, argued, complained, criticized, compared, and were cynical and compulsive. And then in the hour of our Lord's greatest crisis, they all bolted like frightened jackrabbits into hiding.

After Pentecost we see a very different picture. This community of imperfect riffraff was radically transformed. They devoted themselves to gathering together to study Christ's teachings and to pray (Acts 2:42, 44–46). Their love was observable. Like salt, it flavored and preserved their community (Mark 9:49–50). They experienced repeated moves of the Holy Spirit within their congregations (Acts 2:4, 4:31, 13:52). And because this motley band of believers lived the way of the cross, thousands received Christ's gift of forgiveness (Acts 2:41, 4:4, 5:14, 6:7).

As a result, the church was "strengthened and encouraged by the Holy Spirit" and became the talk of the town. Their love for one another consistently confronted the surrounding culture and pioneered social change. The dynamic force of the Spirit among them stunned the known world. This was no quiet curiosity getting a column of type on the back page of Section E in the newspaper. This was headline stuff.

Those on the outside looking in may not have understood early church theology or doctrine, but they recognized love in action when they saw it. Everyone does.

The early church wasn't casual about its commitment to community. These believers were serious about loving God and loving one another. Their devotion was more about conviction than convenience. Why else would they meet together every day, as described in Acts 2:46?

Every day? Pam, are you serious? Yes. Every day. For those of us born and raised in America, this seems rather extreme. Many people view going to church once a week as a "sacrifice" or inconvenience.

In fact, Jesus never said anything about going to church. He called people into community saying, "Let's do life together. Let's pray together, eat together, and talk openly about the things on our hearts. Let's appreciate one another's differences and gifts, and use them to help each other fulfill God's plans in this world."

The Dynamic of His Presence Among Us

Jesus left one thing behind after he rose from the dead and ascended to the Father—a small community of ordinary folks who believed what He said, and tried their best to love one another.

Why did Jesus promote community rather than an independent self-help plan? Like any good teacher, Jesus knew that lecture alone is not enough to transform someone. He understood the dynamics of spiritual growth and change. People have to integrate and practice truth to fully experience it.

It's one thing to know all the nutritional facts about a warm-gooey-hot-fudge-sundae from a book. It's quite another to experience bite after scrumptious bite of this delicious desert with a good friend. In the same way, it's one thing to know about God intellectually, and another to experience His Spirit actively working in and among a group of people who are gathered in His name.

Nothing on earth is more valuable to God than His church. Jesus gave His life for the church. God's presence inhabits the church and marks us off as the people of God, distinguishing us from all other groups on the face of the earth (Exod. 33:15; Eph. 5:18–20; 1 Cor. 3:16).

Gathering as the local church, we experience the dynamic of the Spirit's presence in our midst in a unique way. He speaks to you through me and speaks to me through you. His presence spurs us on in our love affair with God. Like coals in a fire grouped together we generate life-giving energy, and the flames burn higher. When separated from that circle, we grow cold and die out. Community prevents spiritual death and ignites spiritual growth.

Ultimately it boils down to this: When another member of God's family rubs us the wrong way, like coarse sand paper drawn against the grain, we have a choice. We can die to self and yield to the Spirit, or we can yield to self and quench the Spirit (1 Thess. 5:15–19).

When you're struggling with another member of God's family, it might help to remember that God is the only "perfect ten." The rest of us are fives, at best. The ground is level at the foot of the cross. If we want to experience the deeper dimensions of God, we have to quit playing judge and jury and look beyond the limitations and imperfections we see in others.

Stay alert. Don't listen to the voice of the Pharisee. It's more important to love than "to be right."

One afternoon my husband and I were having lunch together. In the course of our conversation he told me how someone had verbally slammed him in front of a group of couples he respected. It wasn't the first time this person had done that sort of thing. I'm not talking about the typical ribbing or poking fun that guys do from time to time. This was a verbal blow beneath the belt that hurt. The pain lingered.

I listened carefully, purposely biting my tongue so I wouldn't throw gas on his fire. After John headed back to work, I fussed and fumed, plopped down on the living room couch and burst into tears. I was so mad I wanted to rip someone's lips off. Ever been there?

"Oh God, I know this grieves You more than it grieves me. I don't want to be bitter, so please, show me what I need to see."

On the heels of that little prayer, within about fifteen seconds, three vivid snapshots flashed sequentially in my mind. In the first freeze-frame I saw myself sitting on the floor with my legs crossed Indian style. Jesus sat across from me in like manner, holding my hands in His. Stroking the top of my hands, He validated my heartache and assured me that He understood. In a split second He changed into an eight-foot warrior who towered over me in full battle attire. Reaching his hands over my head He said, "I've got you covered." Seconds later I saw a picture of our little boy Nathan, hugging the neck of our big chocolate lab Mocha. Nathan's eyes were closed and he was giggling with delight as Mocha licked him all over his face. These words passed through my mind, "I am aggressive in My love for you."

In a brief fifteen seconds my anger plummeted from a ten to a zero. Knowing me, I could have stewed on the issue for days were it not for God's kindness. He met me where I was, in a clump on the living room couch, and poured His love into my heart by the Spirit. As Paul wrote, "Hope does not disappoint us, because God has poured out his love into our hearts by the Holy Spirit, whom he has given us" (Rom. 5:5).

The images I saw in those moments dispelled all fear. Suddenly the offense didn't seem to matter as much. That's the power of God's furious love. It heals.

All-Sufficient Resources

There have been plenty of occasions when I haven't handled things as well and grieved God's Spirit. I've spoken up when I should have shut up. I've said nothing when I should have said something. I've allowed emotion to rule rather than God.

Things would have gone much better had I paused, pondered, and prayed.[2] Remember those three P's the next time you're tempted to give someone a piece of your mind rather than a piece of your heart.

Sitting in the living room, I prayed for John and for the one who had been careless with his words, asking God to mend the rift. As it turned out, a few days later the guys talked, and things were better.

Every community has its share of "difficult" people who tempt us towards strife. We've all brushed shoulders with them: tanks, snipers, exploders, complainers, bulldozers, wet blankets, silent clams, procrastinators, and know-it-alls. If we are honest, we've probably been someone else's difficult person. These are realities of life.

You and I do not have the ability to properly judge relationship conflicts with complete accuracy. We are limited in our understanding, in our courage, and in our ability to respond wisely to the situations that arise.

The good news is the Holy Spirit is our companion, guide, and ongoing power supply. His resources are always sufficient and never ending. The more He fills us, the more we move the cross to the center of our lives. The more we crucify our ego, the more His empowering presence helps us act for the highest good of others— even those who are difficult to love. Like the loaves and fishes in the hands of Jesus, His love multiplies the moment we begin to give it away. There's no better picture of the Spirit of God in community.

Lord, thank You for placing me in Your family. Though I feel alone at times, I am not. There are many wonderful people in my church community. Help me to risk reaching out to them. Grant me courage to share my life. Break down the walls that I've used to fence others out. I open my heart to receive all the blessings You want to give me through others. As I gather with those who love You, speak to me, enlighten me, and meet the needs I can't put into words. And Lord, if there is someone You want to bless, I make myself available to You. Use me to bring Your life-giving hope to others.

CHAPTER 7

THE ONE WHO ANOINTS

Ted Roberts

YOU DON'T HAVE to wait until New Year's Eve to look back over the last twelve months of your life. In fact, you can do it right now. Start at this month, and do a quick flyover back to this time last year.

Is there anything you wish you had done differently? If you had the chance, what would you go back and do over again? And why in the world does it all seem so clear *now* when it seemed so murky and confusing *then*? That's the blessing of twenty-twenty hindsight. A quick glance in the rearview mirror now and then can help you to wisely navigate the present. But just as in driving, if you spend too much time staring in that rearview mirror at where you've been, you're in danger of running yourself right off the road.

You've got some mistakes you regret? Welcome to the human race! We all make mistakes. If you're not making mistakes, you're being way too safe, rather than growing and risking. Mistakes are a necessary part of learning. Please understand this: Your mistakes do not define who you are. Nor do they hold your future hostage.

I firmly believe that no matter where you are in life right now, the best is yet to come. Your best years are ahead. Your biggest joys and God's greatest surprises are in front of you, around the corner, just over the horizon. God is standing in your future, saying, "Come on! Let's go." There's so much for you to look forward to. Mistakes are a launching pad for miracles.

God is more interested in your future than your past. Why? Because you are going to spend the rest of your life in the future! So how can you embrace today, release your mistakes of yesterday, and prepare for your tomorrows? What is God's part and what is your part in fulfilling His plans for your life? *How does the anointing of the Holy Spirit factor in to you becoming all God wants you to be, and achieving all God wants you to achieve?*

The infilling ministry of the Holy Spirit is when the Spirit of God is allowed to freely and richly flow in our lives. In the process, we are empowered to become the man or woman God desires for us to become. The anointing ministry of the Holy Spirit is designed to give us specific abilities and insights to accomplish a task or assignment to which God has called us. Within God's purpose for each of our lives, He has explicit assignments for us to fulfill. And that is why the anointing ministry of the Holy Spirit is so vital in our daily lives.

In the counseling office I frequently encounter sincere, godly folks who are frustrated with life because it "just isn't working." Oftentimes, the problem is obvious: they simply don't understand the anointing ministry of the Holy Spirit. But I usually can't start there. I have to help them through an analysis process about what isn't working in their life before they understand the desperate need we all have for the Holy Spirit's anointing in our lives

One of my jobs in the military was to serve as a safety officer and accident investigator. I didn't realize it at the time, but all the hours I spent studying how and why accidents occurred, actually made me a better pilot. It didn't make me more tentative or hesitant. Fighter pilots who are overly cautious don't survive.

Neither will you, especially if you want experience the fulfillment God has in mind for you! Going deeper with God requires risk and courage. It involves understanding the hows and whys of your mistakes, rather than sweeping them under the rug. So let's do a brief "accident investigation" in your life. If you are anything like the pilots I knew in the military or the folks I've met in the counseling office, your mistakes likely occurred due to one of three reasons.

Mistake One: You Didn't Plan Ahead

Life comes at us with such velocity and vagaries we sometimes make decisions on the spur of the moment, without counting the cost. We neglect taking time to consider the potential consequences of our choices. Scripture frequently warns us of the foolish danger of not planning ahead.

> Wise people think before they act; fools don't and even brag about it!
>
> —PROVERBS 13:16, NLT

Through the years I've met many people who seem to believe that the anointing of the Holy Spirit is primarily a spontaneous experience. They correlate slapdash, spur of the moment activity with Holy Spirit anointing. But the Bible reveals a different picture.

Did Noah suddenly hear the call to build the ark when he was under an umbrella, trying to keep out of the rain? Was Egypt in the middle of a severe drought when Joseph told Pharaoh to start stockpiling grain? Was Jesus surprised by the cross?

The answer to all these questions is an emphatic *no*. God plans ahead and those who walk closely with God and operate in the Spirit's anointing will do the same.

Mistake Two: You Didn't Listen to Others

The Bible says a wise man or woman listens to advice, but a fool thinks he is right (Proverbs 12:15). Why do we close out the counsel of those nearest and dearest to us? Why do we resist wise input from those who deeply care?

There is really only one answer—whether we care to admit it or not, it's pride. And pride, as Solomon made very clear, always precedes a fall.

> Pride goes before destruction, a haughty spirit before a fall.
>
> —PROVERBS 16:18

I believe that verse because it is in God's Word. But do I *like* it? I'm not so sure about that. Last summer I rushed out the front door of our home to go on a bike ride. My racing bike was tuned up and I was excited to see how fast it would go on the open road. As the door slammed behind me, I heard Diane call out, "Honey, don't do anything stupid!" I ignored the silly comment. Good night, we're talking *bicycle* here, not an F-15.

Twenty minutes into the ride I pedaled up a slight hill. Wowed by the speed of the bike I thought, *I'll bet I can hit twenty-five miles-per-hour by the time I reach the top of the hill.* I put my head down and pedaled as hard as I could. One truck passed me on this rural road that typically has very little traffic.

Hunched down low over the front of the bike, I crested the hill and glanced at my speedometer. I was going 25.2 miles per hour! In that instant, something inside said, *Look up.* The second I raised my eyes, I saw the rear end of a parked truck three feet away! I hit that metal tailgate like a bug smashing into a windshield.

Writhing on the side of the road in blinding pain, I heard

the driver say, "Hey buddy, are you all right?" Apparently, he had pulled off the road to make a cell phone call. The only thing over-shadowing the racking pain was the echo of my wife's words, "*Honey, don't do anything stupid.*"

As always, God turned a bad thing into a good thing. The driver started coming to our church and I started listening to my wife. I guess you could call this a creative twist on contact evangelism.

Mistake Three: You Throw in the Towel

The worst mistakes in life happen when we throw in the towel on what truly matters—our marriage, our family, our business, or our ministry. These areas are connected with the deepest dreams and passions of our heart.

I find comfort knowing that great men and women of faith struggle with this same tendency. Paul is probably my all time favorite. He talks openly about his problems, persecutions, perplexities, and pain. He shares a litany of his frustrations, public humiliations, unsuccessful business trips, and apparent failures.

Paul devoted himself to testifying to the Jews that Jesus was the Christ. He was doing precisely what God had told him to do. But throughout the course of his ministry, standing ovations and pats on the back were in short supply. If fact, there was very little acceptance at all—or appreciation, affirmation, or even simple kindness—just resistance and opposition. Actually, the Bible calls it abuse:

> But when the Jews opposed Paul and became abusive, he shook out his clothes in protest and said to them, "Your blood be on your own heads! I am clear of my responsibility. From now on I will go to the Gentiles."
>
> —ACTS 18:6

It looks to me as though Paul had "had enough" of the Corinthian Jews. Had we caught up with him that day outside the synagogue, I think we might have seen a man kicking sand, disgusted with life, apprehensive about the future, and wishing for a different assignment. From the looks of things, he was ready to throw in the towel. That's when the Lord spoke to Paul in a vision: "Do not be afraid; keep on speaking, do not be silent. For I am with you, and no one is going to attack and harm you" (Acts 18:9–10).

After hearing God speak, Paul had a fresh supply of staying power. He had tapped into a source of boundless determination. And the result? "Paul stayed for a year and a half, teaching them the word of God" (Acts 18:11).

Time and again Paul points to the work of the Spirit in his life as the source of his ability to endure. Just when he was ready to throw in the towel because of the mudslinging majority, the political power struggles, and unending exhaustion, the Spirit gave him a glimpse of God's intentions for his life.

Fresh Anointing for New Challenges

My son Brian suffered with terrible food allergies the first few years of his life. We had to be very careful about what we gave him to eat. And yet even with these extra precautions, he continued to react to new foods we tried to introduce into his diet.

By the time Brian was nine years old, I had reached the end of my emotional reserves to deal with the situation. At night he coughed into the wee hours of the morning. The poor little guy couldn't get a decent night sleep, and neither could the rest of us.

I remember when it finally dawned on me that there was a spiritual dimension to his battle. Surely Satan was laughing with glee over disrupting our family night after night. There came a night when I was so exhausted I could barely pray for Brian. My sleep was fitful. In the early morning hours I was abruptly awakened by a sudden sense of an evil presence in our bedroom. Bolting upright, I saw a vicious jackal leering at me at the foot of our bed. Jackals don't live in the Pacific Northwest, so I knew this was a revelation from the Holy Spirit. I rebuked that foul spirit in the name of Jesus.

It withdrew into the shadows, but didn't leave. Adrenaline surged, and I launched an aggressive attack, jumping and shouting, commanding the demonic spirit to leave, and to never return. Diane woke up and thought I was losing my mind. You may be thinking the same thing, too, right about now.

Some things in life defy reason. I knew I was warring against demonic spirits harassing my son, and I wasn't about to back down. In the middle of the fight I sensed the Holy Spirit assuring me that He was healing my son. That still, small voice inside whispered, *A new anointing will rest on you to pray for the sick.*

The victory in Brian's life was glorious! The following day Brian and I went to McDonald's and ordered the biggest strawberry sundae they made. For years dairy products had triggered awful allergic reactions, but not that day.

I will never forget the way his face lit up when that ice cream hit his taste buds. But the best part of the story is Brian never had another allergic reaction to food. Not even one. Like other healthy kids his age, he raided the cupboards and ate us out of house and home.

God has new assignments for you, and a fresh anointing. *What do you mean by anointing?* you ask. That's a great question!

What Does "Anointing" Mean?

The first mention of anointing in the Bible surfaces in a story about Jacob. Remember him? This grandson of Abraham was the first-class con artist who lied to his blind, aged father and twice betrayed his only brother. The name Jacob means "crafty deceiver," and he did a great job living up to his name. Ah, but there came a night.

Do you remember when this son of Isaac slipped through the ropes in the darkness and climbed into the ring with the angel of the Lord? The story tells us that God allowed Jacob to pre-vail—but before He let His man up off the mat, He also dislo-cated Jacob's hip. Let me assure you, friend, a dislocated hip isn't a hangnail or a bad hair day; it's an extremely painful condition. And through all the years of life that followed, Jacob's pronounced limp constantly reminded him that he was not to depend on his own strength. He was to rely entirely on God.

That night when Jacob was alone in the dark, he wrestled with God and God blessed his life. In spite of his seedy track record, in spite of his scheming, manipulative, and deceitful ways, God chose to open heaven's great storehouse and pour His favor out on Jacob. (Why does that encourage me so much?) From that point on, Jacob knew his well-being was dependent on God's power, God's guidance, and God's blessing, not his own devices.

At first light, Jacob got up, stretched, and picked up the stone he had used for a pillow. (I've slept in a few hotels with the same kind of pillows.) The Genesis account tells us that he set up the stone as a pillar and poured oil on top of it. He anointed it, and called the place Bethel which means "the house of God." The loca-tion was previously named Luz which means "almond" (Gen. 28:18–19, AMP).

When God anoints a place, everything about it changes. Jacob revisited Bethel, this sacred place of intimacy with God, many times throughout his life.

When Moses gave instructions about the Tabernacle, he underlined the importance of anointing each object, and every part of the complex (Exod. 30:22–38). After being anointed, this manmade structure became the habitation of God. The lamp stand was no longer an ordinary lamp stand. The tent was no longer a crafted piece of fabric. Every part of the Tabernacle was set apart for God's plans and purposes. It became the place God's presence dwelled.

Fill Every Nook and Cranny

Diane and I have been married thirty-eight years and we have moved seventeen times. With each relocation we anointed the new homes we moved into, declaring the place to be God's house. We wanted God to fill every nook and cranny of each home with His divine presence and to rule and reign in our family.

In a few of the places we rented, this was absolutely critical because previous tenants had apparently welcomed in some very unsavory spirits by their actions and lifestyles. Usually our children would be the first to pick up on the negative spiritual environment. They would begin experiencing disturbing dreams at night. It is normal for children to have troubling dreams at times, but these would be beyond the typical childhood emotional struggles.

These symptoms would provoke Diane and me to prayer, and as we waited on the Holy Spirit, He would direct us as to how we should stand against these spiritual forces. We would simply take a small bottle of olive oil and anoint each room of the house where we sensed demonic activity. Room by room, we declared that this house now belonged to the Lord!

God anoints places, but more importantly, He anoints people. My favorite picture of anointing in the Old Testament is the scene of a diminutive, youthful David being anointed by an aged, impassioned prophet named Samuel. Samuel was deeply grieving King Saul's disastrous failures and departure from God. But God told Samuel to stop weeping because He had found a man after his own heart (1 Samuel 13:14, 16:1).

A young shepherd lad dancing and singing love songs while tending his father's sheep had captured God's attention. God declared, "He is to be the next king of Israel."

Samuel traveled to David's house, spoke with his father Jesse, and informed him that God was going to anoint one of his sons. Jesse introduced each of his sons to Samuel, never considering

David as a possible candidate. He actually referred to David as a *quaton*, which literally means "the runt of the litter."[1]

The good news is God anoints people who you and I would never select if the decision were ours. He picked me! My family wouldn't have picked me. My friends certainly wouldn't have picked me. In fact, I'm the last guy on the planet they would have picked to end up as a pastor. But God had something else in mind. And guess what? God picked you, too.

Maybe you're not supposed to pastor a church, but God picked you to make a difference in this world. He has specific assignments designed especially for you, which only you can complete.

God's anointing brings God's blessing. Being the pastor of East Hill Church has been one of the greatest blessings in my life. As with David, I wasn't looking for it. I assumed I was the most unlikely candidate. But God placed this wonderful gift in my hands anyway—a precious opportunity that has altered the course of my entire life.

The picture of anointing that we find in the Old Testament is a bit different than the one we see in the New Testament. Before Christ's ministry on earth, God poured out His anointing on prophets, priests, and kings. The anointing symbolized their being set apart by God for specific assignments. The anointing came and went.

But in the New Testament we discover the oil of God's anointing, in the Person of the Holy Spirit, is poured out on every believer who decides to follow Christ (Acts 2:17–18). The nature of God's anointing has changed. The Bible tells us that Christ was anointed with the Holy Spirit with power to heal the sick and set the oppressed free (Acts 10:38, NLT).

Penetrating Oil

The word for anointing, *chiro*, is fascinating. It's a picture of oil being smeared upon and rubbed into something.[2] One of the things I enjoy on rare and special occasions is getting a deep sports massage after a tough workout or race. The masseur takes his special oil and works it deep into my fatigued muscles. Without fail I walk out a "new man." The medicinal and relaxing properties of the massage oil work their way down into my flesh. That's chiro.

Chiro is what happens to us in the spirit realm when God anoints us. The Holy Spirit works His way into every space and compartment of our lives that we yield to Him. He penetrates the deep recesses of mind and heart. God literally rubs the oil of His presence into the core of who you are, leaving behind the essence of His nature. Unlike the Old Testament, your anointing doesn't come and go. It's there for good. The Bible says, "As for you, the anointing you received from him remains in you" (1 John 2:27). God anoints and His anointing remains. God rubs it in deep.

The word for anointing in the 1 John passage is the same word used referring to Christ's anointing: chiro! The same God who anointed Christ in the power of the Spirit anoints you. This was God's plan all along.

I know there are many strange folks who act in bizarre ways, claiming to be under the influence of God's anointing. God can and will do odd things at times, but I think sometimes people equate God's anointing with emotion. They err in seeking a sensation rather than the Savior. When the hair on the back of their neck stops standing and the goose bumps fade, they conclude the Holy Spirit's anointing is gone.

Unfortunately, these people end up becoming revival junkies or miracle magnets. It's rather sad because the Bible tells us that God's anointing remains in us. We all experience seasons when we don't feel God's presence, but this doesn't mean His Spirit has left us. It means God is provoking us to go deeper in Him. Like the roots of a tree in a barren desert driving deep towards underground springs, God wants us to progressively press towards new depths of intimacy with Him. The more we move towards God, the more we experience the artesian effect of His life-giving Spirit, bubbling up and out of us like a freshly dug well.

Set Apart for God's Use

God anoints things and He anoints people to set them apart for His use. You have divine assignments no one else can complete. I want to encourage you to keep three things in mind as God massages His Spirit into every aspect of your life.

Be faithful where you are

The anointing that remains in you will impact this world as you are faithful in whatever God asks you to do. He will open new vistas in the Spirit that will both surprise and delight you.

Do you remember Stephen? He was the young man full of the Holy Spirit who was selected by the early disciples to care for the benevolence needs in their community. He assisted widows and waited tables, faithfully conducting his business in a God-honoring way. But that's not all Stephen did.

The Bible tells us this blue-collar worker performed miraculous signs and wonders among the people (Acts 6:1–8). When Stephen was stoned to death for his faith, God opened the eyes of his heart to see into the spirit realm. There before him, in the open heaven, Christ rose to His feet as this first martyr crossed the finish line (Acts 7:56).

Young David was anointed by Samuel to be the next king of Israel. After the anointing service, however, when the prophet had gone home and the excitement died down, the king-elect returned to his dad's flocks out in the boondocks. Anointed or not, he went back to shoveling "sheep stuff." But David was faithful in the little things. As he shoveled one pile of you-know-what after another,

God worked the essence of His nature deep into the fabric of David's life.

My first job in ministry was to load up Teen Challenge teams in my car and drive them throughout the city. During the day, I drove high performance fighter aircrafts. During the night, I was a taxi driver for God. God had already revealed to me that I was called into full time ministry. I think in that brief season of my life He was seeing if I'd be faithful in the little things, before moving me on to other kingdom assignments. He was rubbing the oil of His Spirit into my life.

Next God called me out of the cockpit into the classroom. I spent four long years with my nose buried in books at a theological graduate school. These were years that seemed to last forever, while God worked the oil of His Spirit deep into the wounds and attitudes of my heart.

I'm not the only who has endured God's extreme makeover. After Paul came to Christ, he spent a long season studying God's truth in his hometown, despite the fact that God called him to speak to kings and rulers (Acts 9:15,30). Why did he have to wait so long before being released to fulfill God's assignments? God was working His anointing deep into the thick hide of this bullheaded Pharisees of Pharisees.

Respect and protect the anointing

We can learn an important lesson from King Saul. He had everything going for him. He was smart, talented, and people in high places favored him. When the prophet Samuel anointed Saul, he expressed his affectionate devotion with a kiss (1 Sam. 10:1). Samuel didn't do this for everyone. In fact, as far as we can tell from the Bible, he didn't express this kind of affection towards David.

But the prophet's relationship with Saul "the golden boy" grew increasingly tempestuous over time. Tension built as the two drifted further and further apart. Sometimes our frustration with another individual is a reflection of our deep affection that has been thwarted by that person's lack of maturity.

Eventually the once-promising king flew off the highway of God's goodness, and crashed and burned. I can't imagine the heartache Samuel must have suffered over Saul's demise. How could a man, handpicked by God, have made such catastrophic mistakes—and so quickly?

One of the things I learned in aircraft accident investigation is that tragic crashes are typically the result of something that appears insignificant. During one flight, I instinctively turned my head when I heard the unmistakable sound of ejection seats firing. Behind me, an aircraft slammed into the runway, exploding into a fiery ball of jet fuel and flying metal.

When we investigated the crumpled and charred remains of this powerful aircraft, we discovered the cause of the crash. One small turbine blade in the engine had disintegrated and devoured the engine. A close inspection of the other planes in the squadron was ordered. Sure enough, several other engines also had tiny hairline cracks in their turbine blades. Even though the cracks weren't visible to the human eye, they were potentially deadly.

What brought Saul down? It was the hairline crack in his ego. It was evident from the beginning. Insecurity and inadequacy drove him to destruction. On the gala inauguration day, Samuel brought all the tribes of Israel together to officially appoint Saul as their king. But there was a problem. After searching high and low, they couldn't find the man of the hour. It took God Himself to find the king-elect hiding among the baggage (1 Sam. 10:22). When a bright young warrior by the name of David appeared on the scene, Saul saw nothing but a threat.

The son of Jesse would have undoubtedly served as a loyal and trustworthy lieutenant and friend throughout Saul's reign—if the jealous king would have allowed it. But Saul never fully embraced God's perspective of his own life. He was too busy focusing on David. He compared, competed, criticized, and compulsively tried to control David, rather than keeping his eyes on the faithful execution of his own assignment. The simple song of some happy Israelite women finally sent the obsessive king over the edge.

> But something happened when the victorious Israelite army was returning home after David had killed Goliath. Women came out from all the towns along the way to celebrate and to cheer for King Saul, and they sang and danced for joy with tambourines and cymbals. This was their song: "Saul has killed his thousands, and David his ten thousands!"
> This made Saul very angry. "What's this?" he said. "They credit David with ten thousands and me with only thousands. Next they'll be making him their king!" So from that time on Saul kept a jealous eye on David.
> —1 SAMUEL 18:6–9, NLT

It was so innocent. The women were full of joy for their king and the new Israelite warrior. But Saul looked through the joy and imagined dark threats and conspiracies. But the darkness wasn't in his circumstances; the darkness was in his own heart. The more he believed the lies that fueled his insecurities, the more the power of the Holy Spirit drained from his life.

It can happen to anyone. God got my attention one afternoon when I was listening to a young man tell me about an incredible speaker he had heard. He went on and on and on, praising the man to the skies. Suddenly I felt irritated. I had a nasty urge to share some inside information that I knew about the speaker. It didn't involve blatant sin. It had more to do with the speaker's eccentricities. I had this compulsion to balance my friend's understanding of spiritual leadership. After all, isn't it a fellow believer's duty? Not by a long shot!

The war in my heart, I'm sad to say, wasn't easily won. There was a hairline crack in my ego, threatening the integrity of my interactions with that young man. This particular time, however, I made the right choice, and the story ended on a good note.

Defying the temptation to discredit the speaker, I forced myself to affirm the truth about the man's communication skills.

That's when my friend stopped me mid-sentence. "Pastor Ted," he said, "I just want to thank you for the way you honor others. I grew up in a church where leaders competed with each other. Thanks for your influence in my life." As this young man walked off, I stood there touched by his comments—and deeply convicted about how close I had come to wounding one of God's special people.

Grow in your anointing

David was anointed three different times in his life. The first time happened in the privacy of his own home when Samuel anointed him in the presence of his family. (And what a shocker that was!) The next two anointing ceremonies occurred when he was publicly declared the king of the tribe of Judah, and later king over all of Israel. God gave David a fresh, new anointing when he graduated on to new assignments.

New depths in God await you. Never doubt it! And every new level has a new devil—new problems, new challenges, new dilemmas, and new battles that require a fresh anointing. The early church gives us a picture of how this occurs.

Each time these believers faced new difficulties and opposition, they drew together in community and sought the Lord. Shortly after the day of Pentecost, Peter and John were arrested for healing a crippled man at the temple gate (Acts 4:5–7). The Sanhedrin, similar to our Supreme Court, threatened to execute these two rural fishermen if they continued to speak about Christ. What was their response?

They joined with their fellow believers and had a rip-roaring prayer meeting. Raising their voice in one accord, they declared God's greatness and cried out for Holy Spirit boldness: "Strong God, you made heaven and earth and sea and everything in them. By the Holy Spirit you spoke through the mouths of your servant and our father, David...Give your servants fearless confidence in preaching your Message, as you stretch out your hand to us in healings and miracles and wonders done in the name of your holy servant Jesus" (Acts 4:25, 29–30, THE MESSAGE).

The results were earth shaking—literally. "After this prayer, the building where they were meeting shook, and they were all filled with the Holy Spirit. And they preached God's message with boldness" (Acts 4:31, NLT).

These same believers had been previously filled with the Holy Spirit on the day of Pentecost. On this particular occasion God blessed them with a new anointing to be able to handle the increased opposition and magnitude of their responsibilities.

Chuck is one of the flight instructors that I led to the Lord. Shortly after he opened his heart to Christ, I taught him how to talk with God as he read through the Bible. His faithfulness in this made all the difference in the world on that dreadful day his aircraft smashed into the runway.

When the plane was going down this young warrior ejected from the aircraft microseconds before it hit the tarmac. This saved his life and the life of the student flying with him.

I asked Chuck how he'd made it out alive. He cracked a smile and said, "Well, the morning of the flight when I was reading the Bible, I sensed a warning in my heart to be alert to the landing pattern. It was like God prepared me ahead of time. When the landing started going bad I didn't have time to figure out when to eject. If God hadn't warned me I wouldn't be alive."

Later that month Chuck was asked by the commanding officer to speak to the entire squadron about surviving the crash. Several other pilots had lost their lives that year because they waited too long to eject.

Chuck and I prayed together, asking God to work mightily in that meeting. I watched in amazement as my friend stood before the entire squadron and shared how God prepared him the morning before the engine failure occurred. All ears locked onto the words he spoke. In the coming months Chuck and I had the joy of seeing many of the other instructors accept Christ, along with nearly half of our students. A revival broke out in a fighter squadron! That's about as out of the ordinary as a prayer meeting in a brothel!

But "out of the ordinary" is what life is all about under the anointing of the Holy Spirit.

Heavenly Father, I hunger for a new depth of relationship with You. I yearn for a new level of maturity and fruitfulness in my life. And I freely acknowledge that I can't get there by my own efforts or energy. The dreams and promises You have given me are way beyond me, because they are from You. For this reason, Father, I hunger and thirst for a new level of anointing in life! Come, Holy Spirit, and not only pour over me, but also get down into the cracks and crevices of my soul. Rub the oil down into the little issues and weaknesses within me that most folks can't even see—but one day could rise up and destroy my relationship with you. Help me to guard and protect Your anointing on my life. I choose to agree with You about who I really am, instead of agreeing with my own insecurities or my arrogance. Come, Holy Spirit, and pour over me in a whole new way I pray!

CHAPTER 8

THE ONE WHO WARS
THROUGH US

Ted Roberts

WHEN I RETURNED to the United States after combat duty in Vietnam, I served as a flight instructor for a squadron of young pilots. Since I flew with a land-based unit during my tour overseas, I needed to be recertified in carrier landings.

The Navy scheduled me, along with five other instructors, to jump through the hoops of recertification. This was more of a formality for the other pilots, because they had made scores of carrier landings that year.

All in good fun, they ribbed me unmercifully about how I was going to flunk the test. I did my best to ignore their barbs and lifted the jet off the runway. When the time came to position the aircraft for my first carrier approach, I was surprised to hear a clear voice speaking in my heart. *Ted, how about letting Me flying the plane with you?* God was talking to me. Instantly I blurted out, "Can I still keep my hands on the controls?"

Mind games followed: *Roberts get a grip. You're talking to yourself about God flying this aircraft. Why would He be remotely interested? This is an instrument of war!* I felt like a bloomin' idiot.

Meanwhile, the Holy Spirit patiently waited for my head to catch up with my heart. I'm not sure what drove the decision, wisdom or sheer panic, but I accepted God's invitation: "All right, God. Let's do this assignment together."

To make a long story short, I flew one of the best flights of my life, racking up ten "OK" passes. An "OK" pass means the landing signal officer couldn't find anything wrong with the landing. You have to know the context. These guys do not have a reputation for being gracious. They meticulously scrutinize every detail to the nth degree. Ten OK passes is like playing a round of golf and making a birdie on every hole. God's fingerprints were all over those landings.

The following week when I was reading Scripture, I asked God to help me understand what had happened in the cockpit. These words popped off the page like a flashing neon sign:

> Whatever you do, work at it with all your heart, as work-ing for the Lord, not for men, since you know that you will receive an inheritance from the Lord as a reward. It is the Lord Christ you are serving.
>
> —COLOSSIANS 3:23–24

God was showing me that when I climbed into the cockpit, I wasn't working for my commanding officer, the Marine Corps, or the United States of America. I was working for the Lord.

The Gift of Work

It's the same with you. When you show up at work Monday morn-ing, you're not working for your boss, for the CEO, the manager, or the owner of the business. You are working for God!

The apostle Paul pulls back the curtain of time and describes your job from an eternal perspective. One day you will give an account to a holy God for every aspect of your life. This won't be a time when God assesses whether or not you are good enough to make it into heaven. Christ died for all of our foul-ups, so we don't have to play the ridiculous game of trying to measure up.

This will be a time of receiving rewards. And the greatest reward of all will be the fellowship we share with Christ for all eternity.

Life on this planet is just the beginning. When we die, our work doesn't end. (If you feel like your job is grinding you into dust, hold on. Good news is coming.)

Part of the fun we'll have in heaven includes the work we will be doing with Christ—minus fatigued bodies and discouraged hearts. Several of Christ's teachings vividly underline this truth (Matt. 25:14–30; Luke 19:11–27). When we get to heaven we won't be sitting on clouds strumming golden harps or forced into a never-ending choir practice.

Was flying a high-performance fighter jet exciting? Yes, one of the most exhilarating experiences of my life. Why should I imagine heaven will be less thrilling than that? Maybe on the other side I'll be doing something very similar...minus the jet.

We will be ruling and reigning with Christ. This short life on earth is our training ground for eternity. That's why your work isn't just between you and your boss, or you and your company, or you and your commanding officer. How you carry out your job effects your relationship with God, both now and when you get to heaven.

This was God's plan from the beginning. One of the first gifts God gave man in the Garden of Eden was a job (Gen. 2:15). I've heard some people say that work was a form of punishment God inflicted on Adam and Eve after they sinned. It's as if the world prior to man's sin was like a divine Starbucks, with Adam and Eve hanging out in the garden, smelling flowers, reading their favorite books, and sipping cappuccino nectar. But after they slipped up, God took away their drinks, and assigned them to work the counter or slave in the kitchen. Not even close.

The Bible tells us that when God made everything just the way He wanted it—a perfect world—He gave mankind the responsibility of work. God and Adam shared unbroken intimacy at all times—including the hours Adam was working.

One of the places God wants to cultivate deep intimacy with you is on the job! It doesn't matter where you clock in every day. Whether it's behind a desk or behind a wheel, in your home with your kids or out in the field with a work crew, God wants to do your job with you. The reasons are obvious. The majority of our time is spent working. This is also the primary place we encounter people who have not yet experienced the grace of God.

God encourages us to work for an audience of One:

> Don't just do what you have to do to get by, but work heartily, as Christ's servants doing what God wants you to do. And work with a smile on your face, always keeping in mind that no matter who happens to be giving the orders, you're really serving God. Good work will get you good pay from the Master, regardless of whether you are slave or free. Masters, it's the same with you. No abuse, please, and no threats. You and your servants are both under the same Master in heaven. He makes no distinction between you and them.
> —EPHESIANS 6:5–9, THE MESSAGE

On the heels of these instructions, we find a closing comment about the power God wants to release in and through us on the job. Ephesians 6:10 commands us, "Finally, be strong in the Lord and in his mighty power." The word *power* in the original language is *kratos*, and it carries special significance.[1] It means manifested power that is exerted by a reigning authority. It refers to God's kingdom authority and dominion.[2]

Nothing in this world can match this power. *Kratos* raised Christ from the dead, as the Bible tells us in Ephesians 1:19–20. God wants to release the same power that raised Jesus from the dead in and through you on the job. No wonder I flew the best flight of my life when I handed over the controls!

God doesn't give us His power as an incidental side-benefit when we become a member of His family. He gives us His power because He knows we are virtually inept without it. In fact, we are in great peril.

Life in a War Zone

Let's set the record straight. You and I live in a spiritual war zone. Several of the pilots I worked with didn't enter into a relationship with Christ by coincidence. Diane and I battled in prayer for the souls of these young men and women. It was all out *war*.

I recall a critical turning point when the spiritual climate changed on base. I had heard about a tragic crash involving an Air Force pilot, Chris Mineo. This young warrior was forced to eject from his fighter aircraft just prior to impact. Ejecting from a plane traveling over 700 knots at low altitude is similar to being thrown out of a car going 90 miles per hour and hitting a brick wall!

Chris was severely injured, but in the process of healing he opened his heart to Christ. I sent a letter inviting him to speak to the pilots on base, and he graciously consented to come.

To publicize the event, I made picture posters of an aircraft headed for the ground with a bold caption that read: *What would you do?* I posted ads on the ready room bulletin boards, inviting everyone to come to the meeting. That's when all hell broke loose.

The executive officer of our squadron suddenly took an intense disliking to me. I won't go into the details. Let's just say, the situation wasn't good. He rightly assumed that I was going to share Christ with anyone who came to hear Chris, and it irked him. But I think he was even more irritated that I no longer joined him and the rest of the guys at the bar on Friday nights.

For years I had been in love with alcohol. When I returned to the States following combat the love affair escalated. I was becoming closer to Jack Daniels than to God. Hooked on the stuff, I couldn't seem to break free.

Late one Friday afternoon I drove to the Officer's Club to join some pilots for "Happy Hour." It was our Friday night ritual. We hung out at the bar, told flying stories, and got royally plastered. Friendships were forged in those blurry-eyed conversations. I had a love-hate relationship going with liquor during those days. I loved drinking with the guys, but when I was sober, I knew the alcohol had me in a vise—slowly but surely squeezing the life out of me.

When I got out of my car that afternoon a war broke out in my heart. I began praying in the Spirit (1 Cor. 14:15; Jude 20). My soul cried out to God, speaking in a language I didn't understand, while my feet continued to walk towards the bar. As I approached the door I heard the Spirit say: *Ted, your Father in heaven loves you and accepts you. You don't need to go into the bar again.*

What happened next was an unqualified miracle. I was a full-blown alcoholic—with the scars on my liver to prove it, but when I heard those words I did an about-face, got into my car, drove away, and never touched a drop of alcohol again.

Some of my other struggles took much longer to heal. It was five long years before I escaped the demonic clutches of pornography. In the healing process I learned to walk closely with God and to look to Him daily for deliverance.

Retaking Lost Ground

"Wait a minute, Ted. Are you saying a believer can have a demon?" No. (Besides that, why would you *want* one?) But if you don't think demonic forces can influence believers, you have never been part of a church counsel or committee meeting.

The Bible includes numerous stories about people who were "demon possessed." The Greek word, *diamonizomai*, often translated "demon possessed," is one meaning of the word. It can also mean influence, effect, and hindrance.[3] There are varieties of demonic activity that affect human beings other than full possession.

The Bible says that one of the specific reasons Jesus came to this earth was to destroy the works of the devil (Matt. 12:28; 1 John 3:8). On the cross, Christ defeated the devil, and all the evil spirits working with him. Having disarmed the powers and authorities, he made a public spectacle of them, triumphing over them by the cross (Col. 2:15).

My friend, Jesus has given you and me the spiritual authority to enforce His victory in this world (Matt. 28:18; Luke 10:19). We are to wage war in the Spirit and take back any ground the enemy has encroached upon or stolen.

Perhaps a picture will help explain Christ's ministry of deliverance. Let's look at the different ways demonic activity can affect people. In the chart below you see something that looks a little bit like the old "X and Y" chart from high school algebra. Don't worry. This isn't a math equation. It's simply a graphic representation of how demonic forces strategize against human beings.

A Deliverance Model

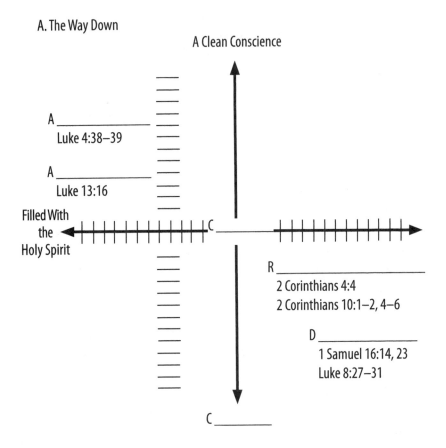

The upper left hand corner of the chart is the place God has designed us to live. We experience the abundant life He promised when we live with a clear conscience, full of the Holy Spirit. This is where we experience the deepest level of meaning, purpose, and satisfaction in this world. The bottom right hand side of the chart is the place where Satan tries to lure us to live—a condemned, compulsive, and crippled state, dominated by dark forces. Between these two extremes, there is a wide array of human experience.

Simon Peter's mother-in-law was serving the disciples and

suddenly came down with a high fever. Jesus didn't pray for her healing. Instead, He *rebuked* the fever and it left her. In the original text Christ literally commands the wicked spirit to "shut up!" (Luke 4:38–39). He uses this same language in other demonic confrontations (Mark 1:25; Matt. 17:18; Luke 9:42).

Are you wondering, "How can a demonic spirit influence such a kind, godly woman?" The answer is, *easily*. It is what he does. We live in fallen world and Satan is the ruler of this world (John 12:31, 14:30). This present evil age lies under the sway of the wicked one (Gal. 1:4, NKJV; 1 John 5:19, NKJV). Anyone can be harassed by his wicked schemes at any time. However, let's be clear about the truth: "He who is in you [the Holy Spirit] is greater than he [the devil] who is in this world" (1 John 4:4).

One day Jesus was teaching in the synagogue. A woman attending the service was bent over, unable to stand up straight. The story says she had suffered eighteen years with this physical problem. Luke, the physician, explained that a crippling spirit caused the condition. Seeing the woman's agony, Jesus called her to join Him. It was customary in that day for women to sit separate from men, typically in a balcony. Jesus honored the woman when He invited her to stand among the men with Him.

Gently placing His hands on her, He called her, "daughter of Abraham." This was one of the highest compliments a Jewish woman could receive. Immediately the woman stood straight and tall, free from *eighteen years* of crippling shame.

Taking Out Enemy Bunkers

One of Satan's favorite strategies is to capitalize on our weaknesses and vulnerabilities. He delights in rubbing our noses in our inadequacies and dishing out accusations. There is good reason (Rev. 12:10). Tempting us into shame is one of his more common tactics. Reminding us of our past mistakes, he sets up an intravenous drip-drip-drip of lies. Stirring up the painful memories of our wounds, he tempts us to buy into ideas that *are not true*. These lies become like "fortresses" in our mind, restricting our ability to respond freely to the Holy Spirit.

The Bible says, "For though we walk in the flesh, we do not war according to the flesh. For the weapons of our warfare are not carnal but mighty in God for pulling down strongholds, casting down arguments and every high thing that exalts itself against the knowledge of God, bringing every thought into captivity to the obedience of Christ" (2 Cor. 10:3–5, NKJV).

The word "stronghold," *ochuroma*, graphically pictures both a fortress and a prison. In ancient civilization a stronghold was a place surrounded by huge, impregnable walls. Within that fortress was a prison, or a place of detention and restriction.

There are parallels in the spirit realm. Satan's strategy is to exert power over us through lies. These carefully calculated falsehoods are like prison bars that hold us hostage. Viewing life from behind these bars distorts reality. A downward spiral ensues. Lies lead to distortions. Distortions lead to destruction. For years I believed I couldn't live with out a drink. Held captive by this lie, I was slowly poisoning myself.

As I prayed in the Spirit on my way into the bar, it was as if the Holy Spirit flipped on the lights. I saw the lie, heard the truth, and was assured deep within that I was totally accepted and loved by my heavenly Father. That truth—*the* truth—set me free.

Deliverance is often needed to break free from the pain that drives our compulsions. I'm not talking about "Hollywood style" deliverance, complete with contortions, screaming, and frothing at the mouth. The Holy Spirit often moves gently and tenderly to set people free.

Sometimes it looks similar to what He did for me, when He gave me insight and energized me to walk away from temptation. He removes blinders from our eyes and shows us truth that doesn't fit our logic or former view of things. It can take a while for our spiritual eyes to adjust to what God exposes in the light of His presence, but eventually things come into focus.

Tears sometimes reflect a newfound liberty. In order to break the chains of spiritual bondage we need more than a strong will. We need the resurrection power of the Holy Spirit to blast through our mental jail cells and usher us into freedom.

Firefight

Satan's goal is to dominate you. We've spoken of King Saul in previous chapters. Early on in his life he enjoyed God's imminent presence. The Holy Spirit came upon him and caused him to prophesy (1 Sam. 10:5–11). He empowered Saul to conquer his enemies. But during the second year of his kingship, Saul chose to completely disregard God's instructions. Disobedience was his downfall, and it cost him dearly. The Spirit of the Lord departed from Saul, and a distressing spirit harassed him. Demonic forces capitalized on Saul's insecurities, driving him to persecute young David, to seek counsel from a spirit medium, and eventually to take his own life.

Scripture tells us about another demon-possessed man who lived in some tombs in the region of the Garasenes. We don't know how the devil gained ground in this man's life, but we do know that a legion of demons controlled him. When Christ stepped out of the boat onto the shore, the man came out of the tombs screaming at Jesus.

Jesus commanded the legion of evil spirits to come out of the man. Instantly he was freed from the forces that had countermanded his own rational powers and physical actions. Clothed and in his right mind, this man became the very first missionary to the Gentiles, long before the apostle Paul ever heard the call of Christ (Luke 8:26–39).

Can you see why being continually filled with the Holy Spirit is an absolute necessity? How else will you be able to discern and counteract demonic forces that strategize against you?

Deep communion with God must be continual because spiritual warfare is ongoing. Victory over dark forces is won by the power of the Spirit in you, aggressively waging war through you.

Breaking Stony Hearts

To return to my story about Chris Mineo, the injured young fighter pilot I had invited to speak to our squadron, the event took place on schedule—despite the Executive Officer's opposition. In keeping with squadron policies, we held the meeting during off-duty hours, and I had no idea how many people would show up.

Before the meeting, Diane and I, along with several friends, sat in our car passionately praying for all those that would attend the event. The Holy Spirit spoke to one of these prayer warriors and said, "I will break stony hearts."

As it turned out, the meeting was packed with pilots from three squadrons. Chris shared his story, balancing himself with a cane. One of his legs was still in bad shape. He talked of God's love in a way that made sense to folks who didn't attend church.

About the time he was going to close the evening with prayer, a woman in the back of the room suddenly stood up and began to speak in tongues. She promptly interpreted what she had said in tongues, in English, and then sat down. A stunned silence engulfed the room. I was in shock. Chris handed the meeting back to me saying something like, "You've got it Ted."

Diane encouraged me to not apologize for what had just happened. She sensed God was using the situation, because part of the woman's message was, "God is breaking stony hearts."

I made my way to the front of the room, mumbled something about the fact that what had just happened was in the Bible, and then dismissed everyone. The group almost trampled one another, making a bee-line for the back door.

I found out later the mystery lady in the back of the room was visiting a friend from another part of the country. Apparently they ended up at our meeting purely "by accident."

Diane and I had prayed for months for four specific couples on base that did not know Christ. And it was these very four couples who lingered to talk with Chris after the meeting, opening their hearts to Christ.

On the way out of the building I turned to one of the guys and asked, "What did you think about the lady that spoke in tongues?"

His response caught me completely off guard: "Ted, we weren't planning on staying for the entire meeting. We were going to slip out early in order to get to another party, but when that lady stood up and began to speak in tongues, I knew God was in the room and I couldn't leave."

The Bible tells us that the gift of public tongues is a sign for unbelievers, not for believers. I witnessed the beauty of this gift in living Technicolor that night (1 Cor. 14:22).

As you might expect, I received a lot of flak at work the next day. One young buck came up to me and said, "Ted—you guys really put on a show last night. What the ____ was that woman doing?"

I smiled and shot back, "Yep, it was quite a show. Glad you could make it." He happened to be sitting right next to our mystery guest that night. God definitely got his attention. I doubt he'll ever forget the evening.

The Double-Edged Sword

The person of the Holy Spirit passionately desires to war through you for the hearts of lost men and women. Words cannot express how much people matter to God. One of the most effective weapons in His arsenal is the weapon he placed in our hands that night. God provides a detailed description of the armament available to you, highlighting one strategic offensive weapon. He says:

144 | Going Deeper

> Take the helmet of salvation and the sword of the Spirit, which is the word of God. And pray in the Spirit on all occasions with all kinds of prayers and requests. With this in mind, be alert and always keep on praying for all the saints.
>
> —Ephesians 6:17–18

We are told to take up the *machaira*, or, double edged sword.[4] The Roman army was unbeatable because they had mastered the use of this weapon at close range.[5] When a Roman soldier engaged in combat, he punched his enemy in the face with a shield and then stabbed him in the stomach with his double edged sword. Paul is trying to help us understand that God doesn't want us taking a static defensive posture in spiritual warfare. He wants us to aggressively deliver devastating blows to the enemy.

What makes this sword lethal? It's two razor-sharp edges: The spoken word of God and praying in the Spirit.

A quick look at the original language helps shed light on what Paul means when he says, "Take…the sword of the Spirit, which is the *word of God*; praying always with all prayer and supplication in the Spirit" (Eph. 6:17–18, NKJV, emphasis added).

Paul's word choice is strategic. The Greek term used for "word" is *rhema*. *Rhema* refers to a spoken word that is specific for the need of the moment.[6] It is different from logos, which refers to Scripture as a whole. *Rhema* is a specific word of truth, which the believer wields as a sword in battle, according to the need. When Christ was tempted by Satan in the desert He said, "It is written, Man shall not live by bread alone, but by every word (*rhema*—specific spoken word) that proceeds from the mouth of God."[7]

The words used in the original Greek for "praying in the Spirit" also emphasized the specific need of the moment. Prayer in this warfare text is *proseuchomai*, which refers to a petition arising out of a necessity.[8]

When Diane and I prayed with our friends in the car before the meeting on base, the Holy Spirit spoke a *rhema* word to us—a promise for the need of the moment. It was a specific word that identified what God intended to do that night. He said He was going to break stony hearts. We received the word and guarded it by praying in the Spirit.

God confirmed His *rhema* word to us through the woman who spoke in tongues and interpreted her message in English. We saw God do what He said He was going to do. Stony hearts were broken. God demolished the fortresses and rocky encasements hell had constructed around human hearts, and four couples entered into a personal relationship with Christ.

I'm very well aware that the subject of "speaking in tongues" has been a controversial issue in the American church during the last fifty years. Some say it has split churches. (But then, so has arguing over the color of the new carpet or whether to allow drums in the sanctuary. If people have a mind to argue, they will find *something* to argue about.) When I travel in third world countries, however, this so-called "controversial issue" isn't controversial at all. It's simply a part of normal Christian life. In many of these nations, the supernatural is embraced as an expected, natural part of a believer's daily walk.

I believe there is a fresh wave of faith in America, particularly among young people who are sold out for God. I sense even greater change on the horizon. Peter Wagner, founding president of Global Harvest Ministries, and co-founder of the World Prayer Center, recently said that except for a diminishing number of Christians who say the miraculous gifts of the Spirit have ceased, there is widespread acceptance among believers that speaking in tongues is a bona fide gift of the Holy Spirit.[9]

A careful study of Scripture, particularly Paul's letters, reveals that the gift of tongues can be used privately, between an individual and God, or publicly, for the benefit of a corporate gathering of believers. When we speak privately in tongues, we are speaking to God and not to man. It is a gift that can deepen our intimacy with God. I'm going to take the risk of including an extended passage of

146 | GOING DEEPER

Scripture here. Please don't skim through the following passages
from Eugene Peterson's *The Message*. I know you'll find them well
worth your while!

> Give yourselves to the gifts God gives you…If you praise
> him in the private language of tongues, God understands
> you but no one else does, for you are sharing intimacies just
> between you and him. But when you proclaim his truth in
> everyday speech, you're letting others in on the truth so that
> they can grow and be strong and experience his presence
> with you. The one who prays using a private "prayer lan-
> guage" certainly gets a lot out of it, but proclaiming God's
> truth to the church in its common language brings the
> whole church into growth and strength. I want all of you to
> develop intimacies with God in prayer, but please don't stop
> with that. Go on and proclaim his clear truth to others.
>
> So, when you pray in your private prayer language,
> don't hoard the experience for yourself. Pray for the insight
> and ability to bring others into that intimacy. If I pray in
> tongues, my spirit prays but my mind lies fallow, and all
> that intelligence is wasted. So what's the solution? The
> answer is simple enough. Do both. I should be spiritually
> free and expressive as I pray, but I should also be thought-
> ful and mindful as I pray. I should sing with my spirit, and
> sing with my mind…I'm grateful to God for the gift of
> praying in tongues that he gives us for praising him, which
> leads to wonderful intimacies we enjoy with him. I enter
> into this as much or more than any of you.
> —1 CORINTHIANS 14:1–5,13–18, THE MESSAGE

Paul reveals the place of tongues in his own personal prayer
life. Praying in the Spirit does not engage the intellect. Singing
and praying with his intellect, and in the Spirit, was a normal part
of Paul's life. There is absolutely no hint of emotionalism, hype, or
unusual behavior of any kind. The use of tongues was one of the
ways Paul cultivated deep intimacy with God and won spiritual
battles (Eph. 6:18).

The Bible places no restrictions on the personal, devotional use of tongues. On the other hand, there are clear restrictions on the public use of tongues, spelled out in Scriptures such as 1 Corinthians 14:5, 9, 13, and 39.

Our focus here is on how the Holy Spirit wants to work in and through you in the marketplace, outside the gathering of the local church. This is where private tongues can be extremely empowering. The Word of God, combined with a personal prayer language is a double-edged sword for conquering enemies in the spirit realm.

Breakthroughs

I've shared several breakthroughs that happened in my life as a result of praying in the Spirit. Through using my prayer language I was set free from the violent flashbacks I suffered following combat in Vietnam. On another occasion this weapon won a battle in the spirit realm, which resulted in my son's healing. I firmly believe that situations on the job, particularly things over which I had no control, were influenced as the Holy Spirit prayed through me. The turnaround I witnessed on base was nothing short of supernatural. There are many more stories I could tell you if we both had more time.

I remember my first encounter with tongues in a public worship service. The experience seemed strange and uncomfortable. It left me feeling unsettled, because I didn't know what God's Word said on the subject. I spent considerable time investigating Bible passages that mentioned tongues, seeking to understand the role this gift played in the early church.

In the Book of Acts, speaking in tongues often accompanies the infilling of the Holy Spirit. Notice I said *often*. I did not say *always*. God, in His kindness, doesn't make any of His gifts a "have to." He is a gentleman and never forces anything on anyone.

When people ask, "Pastor, do I have to speak in tongues to be filled with the Holy Spirit?" I have one response. "No, you *get* to!"

I'm not trying to be trite. I am trying to underline the fact that a private prayer language is another way you can take your relationship with God to new depths. It is spirit-to-Spirit communion, where your spirit connects intimately with the Holy Spirit.

Are there ever times when you just don't know how to pray? (I just asked you if you have a pulse.) These are the moments that are custom designed for the Holy Spirit to do His greatest work.

I remember the years my children were growing up. I didn't have a clue how to be a godly dad. Believe me, the six stepfathers that came and went did not model good parenting skills. I was terrified that I'd fail as a father. During those child-rearing years I learned to pray in the Spirit as never before. The Holy Spirit cried out through me to God, expressing and sorting through the confusion I couldn't explain with words.

> In the same way the Spirit also helps our weakness; for we do not know how to pray as we should, but the Spirit Himself intercedes for us with groanings too deep for words; and He who searches the hearts knows what the mind of the Spirit is, because He intercedes for the saints according to the will of God.
>
> —ROMANS 8:26–27, NASB

These were years of deep intimacy with God and deep healing in my soul. Now as a grandfather, I use my prayer language daily. I've learned that good grandparents show up and keep unsolicited parenting advice to themselves. I love on the grandkids whenever I can, and frequently pray in the spirit to wage war on their behalf.

Sometimes when I am talking with God, I sense the Holy Spirit wants to pray through me for a situation or person. By faith, I yield my tongue to Him. Please remember, we are saved by faith, sanctified by faith, transformed by faith, *and we use spiritual gifts by faith.*

There is nothing sensational, sudden, or weird about using a private prayer language. It is a willful decision experienced by faith. I typically don't know what the Holy Spirit is praying through me, but I have complete confidence in His ability to translate whatever I say into an instrument of war that wins spiritual battles and accomplishes other kingdom objectives.

I've wondered if He says something like, "Father, you know all about Ted's concerns. You've heard every one of his prayers. I know he has asked You for such and such, but what he *really* needs is..." I don't envision Him being pejorative. I see Him just looking out for me. As the wonderful Counselor, He knows all, sees all, and always has my best interests in mind.

Why the Gift of Tongues?

Have you ever wondered why speaking in tongues is often mentioned in Scripture with being filled with the Holy Spirit? I sure have. I know that God is God, and that He can do anything He wants. I also know that God is not indiscriminate, random, or arbitrary in His actions. Even so, when I was younger in my faith, I had a hard time grasping the relevance of this gift. It just didn't make sense to me.

The intellectual struggle continued until I learned something fascinating about the speech mechanics of the brain. The ability to communicate with language sets man apart from all other living things. Of all God's creatures, man alone possesses this ability. Speech and language requires over 50 percent of the brain's use. This is higher than any other single activity.[10] Walking, seeing, smelling, or even abstract thinking does not involve as much of the brain.

The first recorded activity of man in Scripture involved speech. God told Adam to name the animals. Now catch this next point. The reason that speech involves so much of the brain is because the language processing sequence isn't simply a matter of memory recall. It involves a complex mental feedback loop.[11] When you are looking for a word to express a thought or idea, your brain doesn't simply select a word stored in a single mental file. Using a rough analogy, your mind seeks through video libraries in multiple parts of the brain.

A number of missionaries have told me that they knew the native language of the people they had been called to serve was sinking in when they started dreaming in that language during sleep. I have also stood at the bedside of Spirit-filled stroke patients. Though they had lost their capacity to speak in English, they could still pray in the Holy Spirit.

Praying in the Spirit activates multiple parts of the brain, and is not impaired when linear reasoning processes are hindered. Praying in the Spirit can work like a spiritual "anti-virus" or "defrag process" that deep-cleans our mental computer, dumping unnecessary clutter. No wonder God led me to pray in the Holy Spirit when I was experiencing violent flashbacks of war. No wonder Paul tells us to "pray in the Spirit on all occasions." Perhaps this explains why I hear God speak words of wisdom and knowledge when I'm praying in the Spirit. It's as if my prayer language clears the static in the spirit realm, and fine-tunes my ears to more clearly hear His voice.

Is it strange? Is it magic? Is it imaginary? Is it out-on-the-fringe mystical? Is it over-the-top emotional? No to all the above. Praying in the Spirit, the gift of tongues, is a spiritual discipline, used in faith, where God works in ways beyond linear thought and human logic.

In the tiny Book of Jude, verse 20 has a blockbuster promise about praying in the Holy Spirit. It says, "But you, dear friends, carefully build yourselves up in this most holy faith by praying in the Holy Spirit" (THE MESSAGE).

Does your faith need fortifying? Does your soul need strength? Does your will need some wonder-working power? It's yours to receive as you pray in the Spirit.

How did the executive officer react to our meeting with Chris

Mineo? I'll sum it up this way. Standing at rigid attention in front of his desk, I quietly prayed in the Spirit under my breath. I expected him to spew a string of colorful expletives, while slicing and dicing my existence.

Instead, he looked up from the paper on his desk with a pained expression on his face. Then, slowly taking a pen in hand, he signed his name to the bottom of what looked like a formal document. I suspected they were court martial papers, even though I had done nothing to deserve that kind of treatment. He was so hostile toward me that I figured he would find some way to get rid of me.

I couldn't help but hear the strain in his voice when he said, "I can't believe I am signing this thing, Roberts. The commanding officer nominated you for Instructor of the Year and asked me to endorse the recommendation!"

Apparently orders had been given from those in higher places to improve community relations. The Vietnam War had been both unpopular and controversial. The military was looking for ways to cultivate a more positive public image. When nominees were being considered, community service was a top priority. The work I had done with Teen Challenge was right in line with their awards criteria.

Obviously distressed, the executive officer nearly broke his pen signing that letter of recommendation. I stood silent, stunned and warmed all over by God's marvelous grace. The famous words of Psalm 23 danced in my soul:

> You prepare a banquet for me where all my enemies can see me...I know that your goodness and love will be with me all my life.
>
> —PSALM 23:5–6, GNT

Heavenly Father, I admit at times I don't even know how to pray. And at times I am struggling too deeply to pray effectively—my mind pulled in so many directions. But

I'm going to step forth in faith, trusting the Holy Spirit to pray through me. I yield my heart, my soul, and my tongue to You. Come and cleanse, clarify, and cut through the junk in my life as only You can. I want to make a difference on the job, in my home, and in this world for You, Lord!

APPENDIX:
LET'S GO DEEPER

Chapter 1:
The One Who Seals

A treasure to keep

If you have said yes to Christ, the Person of the Holy Spirit lives within you, and wants to personally lead you into a deeper experiential intimacy with God.

A verse to embrace

> [He] set his seal of ownership on us, and put his Spirit in our hearts as a deposit, guaranteeing what is to come.
> —2 Corinthians 1:22

A time with friends

This book was designed for you to read and experience with friends. We urge you to invite others to join you on your adventure to go deeper with God. After an initial "ice-breaker" to open up discussion, we'll include several questions that will aid your small group in discussing the contents of each chapter.

***

Describe a Jacques Cousteau-type experience when you were physically or emotionally "in so deep" that your "lips began to tremble uncontrollably and your spine bend backward like a bow." How did you get through it?

Let's dive deeper

Beginning scuba divers don't enter the water without a dive coach. They are cautioned to never dive alone. God offers you His Spirit to be your coach and guide. Have you said yes to Christ, and been sealed by the Spirit?

If you have, what difference has the Holy Spirit made in your life? Please share these thoughts with your small group.

If anyone in your group has not received Christ, please pause and pray for the Holy Spirit to begin His work in their lives.

God has unlimited resources at your disposal. How do you need Him to resource you today? What is one of your pressing needs?

Ask each person in your group to identify one pressing need. Make a list of those needs, and then take some time to pray and ask God to meet them. When you meet together again next week, share with each other how God answered these prayers.

What is one treasure you discovered on our journey through this study with your friends?

What would you attempt for God if you knew you couldn't fail? (Reminder: the power of the Holy Spirit will never fail you. You are sealed by Him.)

Chapter 2:
 The One Who Reveals

A treasure to keep

The Person of the Holy Spirit longs to reveal God's perspectives, which are beyond natural human reasoning. He will show you what you need to see and empower you to act with wisdom in your daily life.

A verse to embrace

> I keep asking that the God of our Lord Jesus Christ, the glorious Father, may give you the Spirit of wisdom and revelation, so that you may know him better. I pray also that the eyes of your heart may be enlightened in order that you may know the hope to which he has called you, the riches of his glorious inheritance in the saints, and his incomparably great power for us who believe.
>
> —Ephesians 1:17–19

A time with friends

Describe a time in your life when you experienced God's presence with you. How did He assure you He was there?

Let's dive deeper

The Scriptures, inspired by the Holy Spirit, are the written revelation of God. God reveals Himself in His Word. As you read the passages of Scripture in this chapter, what is one new insight you gained about God? Please share these insights with your small group. Record the insights others gained while reading these passages.

As you read the stories in this chapter, did any memories surface of ways God has given insight and wisdom to you or to loved ones? Please share these stories with your small group.

The Spirit of wisdom and revelation is passionate about giving you everything you need for life in this world. Identify an area in your life where you need insight and wisdom. Share these needs with your group. Make a list of all the needs represented in the group and pray together for each individual.

When you meet together next week, share with each other what the Holy Spirit revealed to you during the week. How did you act on what He showed you?

The busyness and noise of this world often drowns out the

voice of the Holy Spirit within you. Identify three specific times this week when you will shut out the noise and spend time with God. Write those days and times below. Be accountable to the group next week by sharing how God revealed Himself to you during these quiet moments.

Chapter 3:
The One Who Empowers

A treasure to keep

The Holy Spirit always strives for unity. His empowering presence inhabits communities that function as one.

A verse to embrace

> If two of you agree on earth concerning anything that they ask, it will be done for them by My Father in heaven. For where two or three are gathered together in My name, I am there in the midst of them.
>
> —Matthew 18:19–20, nkjv

A time with friends

Share with the group a memory of when you had some great fun with someone else.

Let's dive deeper

In this chapter we said, "Like coals in a fire grouped together, we generate life-giving energy and fan one another into flame. When separated from the circle, we grow cold and die out. Community prevents spiritual death and ignites spiritual growth."

At what point in your life were you most on fire for God? What fanned the flame?

At what point in your life did your flame for God almost flicker out? What doused the flame?

Are you listening to the voice of the Pharisee in any of your relationships? Share briefly how you would like the group to pray for you about this.

What will you do to ensure you don't grieve the Spirit who lives in your heart?

What is one step you will take this week to protect a spirit of unity in your family and your church community? Share this with your group.

Ask God to give you the name of one person He would like to reach out to this week. Ask Him how He would like you to extend yourself. Then do it.

Chapter 4:
The One Who Releases

A treasure to keep

The Holy Spirit releases His power in and through your weaknesses.

A verse to embrace

> If you then, being evil, know how to give good gifts to your children, how much more will your heavenly Father give the Holy Spirit to those who ask Him.
> —LUKE 11:13, NKJV

A time with friends

Share with the group a story of a miracle you have heard some time in your life.

Let's dive deeper

What assignment seems way too big for you? In what area of your life are you overwhelmed, at the end of your resources, needing God's supernatural power? Share these needs around the circle. Notice the differences and similarities in the needs expressed.

What miracle would you like to ask God to perform for another member of your group? Pray as a group for each person.

Ask God to release His miracle working power into the center of their need.

Chapter 5:
The One Who Transforms

A treasure to keep

God uses your struggles to get your attention so that He can heal and transform you.

A verse to embrace

> And we, who with unveiled faces all reflect the Lord's glory, are being transformed into his likeness with ever-increasing glory, which comes from the Lord, who is the Spirit.
> —2 CORINTHIANS 3:18

A time with friends

Share with the group what action adventure actor or actress you would like to have portray yourself in a film about your life and the hang ups you have come through.

Let's dive deeper

What hang up or hook has the Lord helped you get free from in the past? And what was the turning point for you? If it was an issue that you struggled with for years, why was the battle so long? After you share with others, listen carefully as they share and see if there are any common patterns in your experiences. If there were common patterns, what do those patterns tells us about the Holy Spirit's ministry in our lives?

How has the Holy Spirit gotten your attention through the tough times you have gone through? What have you learned about God's love for you? What have you learned about the transformation process he is taking you through?

As the group shares about the ways the Holy Spirit has gotten their attention during the tough times of life what facets of

God's character are revealed by their experiences? How have friends made the difference in your life when you felt like you weren't going to make it? What types of friends are the most helpful to you in this tough transformation process Christ is taking you through? How can you grow into being a friend with those character traits in your life?

Take some time to ask if any one in the group is presently going through a tough time and then pray for them expecting the Holy Spirit to speak through you to bring comfort to their soul.

Chapter 6:
The One Who Unites

A treasure to keep

The Holy Spirit co-labors with you in the transformation process to leave Christ's imprint on your generation.

A verse to embrace

> Do not conform yourselves to the standards of this world, but let God transform you inwardly by a complete change of your mind. Then you will be able to know the will of God—what is good and is pleasing to him and is perfect.
> —ROMANS 12:2, GNT

A time with friends

What kinds of people do you have a difficult time being patient with? Why do they get to you? Where and when do you get impatient with yourself? Why do you get to yourself at times?

Let's dive deeper

Sometimes we just react to things. What kinds of overreactions are common for you? What lights your fuse? On a sheet of paper, list the things that can trigger you in life. Then pause for a moment and ask God the Holy Spirit to show you if there are any patterns of reactions in your life.

What are the areas where you find it hard to believe God at times? Where do you tend to struggle in your faith (remember that is not a sin)? You can't really have faith without doubts. In your area of doubt, where does God want to bring faith? How do you think he desires to do that in your life? What responses to do you need to make, one decision at a time?

What are some Holy Spirit disciplines you need to grow in so that the renewing of your mind can really deepen? The examples given were worship, memorizing scripture, praying in the Holy Spirit—which of these could be growth areas for you?

Where, specifically, has God called you to be a generation changer? If you are not sure, ask your small group to pray with you and over you. Listen carefully to what takes place. Expect a life-changing word from God to resound in your soul!

Chapter 7:
The One Who Anoints

A treasure to keep

God wants to massage the anointing oil of His Holy Spirit deeply into the essence of who you are.

A verse to embrace

> But they're no match for what is embedded deeply within you—Christ's anointing, no less!
> —1 JOHN 2:27, THE MESSAGE

A time with friends

Give each person a playing card in your group and point out that every person is dealt a different hand in life—family of origin, financial resources, stressors, etc. Ask the members of the group to break up into smaller groups of 3 to 4 people and have them describe the cards they have been dealt in life—aces, jokers, whatever.

Then call the group back together and point out that whatever cards they may have been dealt in life—they get to choose how they are played. And God the Holy Spirit can always give us a trump card in our life, no matter what problems we face.

Let's dive deeper

In the areas pointed to as possible causes for mistakes being made in our life, which one has been a struggle for you? Not planning ahead? Not listening to the advice of others? Throwing in the towel? How have you been able to grow in that struggle point in your life? What have you found that helps you not fall into the trap of making the same mistakes again in your life?

When have you experienced a new sense of the Holy Spirit's anointing in your life? What led up to that experience? What changed in your life with that new sense of anointing?

Where do you just need to be faithful in the anointing you presently have? How have you learned to protect that anointing? Have you ever had a struggle like the one mentioned in the chapter of getting mentally caught up in comparison? How did you avoid grieving the Holy Spirit?

Where do you need a new level of anointing in your life right now? Have your small group pray for that to take place in your life.

Chapter 8:
The One Who Wars Through Us

A treasure to keep

God is your boss, and He wants to release the supernatural through you in the marketplace.

A verse to embrace

> At the same time the Spirit also helps us in our weakness, because we don't know how to pray for what we need. But

the Spirit intercedes along with our groans that cannot be expressed in words.

—ROMANS 8:26, GWT

A time with friends

What is the funniest, or the wildest, or the most embarrassing thing that has ever happened to you on the job?

Let's dive deeper

How have you discovered that Jesus is really the boss on your job?

How can you grow in experiencing that truth in your life at a deeper level?

What are your thoughts concerning the fact that heaven is not about sitting on a cloud but working with Christ in eternity? Working in an environment where there is no sin, no prejudice, no back biting; what will that be like?

Where have you encountered God's "mighty strength" on the job?

Where have you experienced a spiritual war zone on your job?

Have you ever had to work with someone, like the executive officer that opposed and oppressed you?

How did God help you handle the pressure?

Have you ever encountered the demonic in this fallen world? How did the Holy Spirit help you to deal with the enemy?

What were your thoughts about "tongues" before reading this chapter?

How did the chapter influence your view of tongues?

When has God placed that double-edged sword of a rhema and praying in the Spirit in your hands? What were the results?

If you have a "private prayer language" how has it helped you in the daily struggles of life?

NOTES

INTRODUCTION
The Fire of His Love

1. Blaise Pascal, "Memorial," in *Great Shorter Works of Pascal*, (Philadelphia: The Westminster Press, 1948), 117.

CHAPTER 1
The One Who Seals

1. Robert Sullivan and Robert Andreas, *The Greatest Adventures of All Time* (Des Moines, IA: Time, Inc., 2000), 28–32.

2. Ibid.

3. Jack Hayford, *The Spirit Formed Life* (Ventura, CA: Regal Books, 2001), 54.

4. R. A. Torrey, *Why God Used D. L. Moody* (New York: Fleming H. Revell Company), 51–55.

CHAPTER 2
The One Who Reveals

1. J. B. Phillips, *Ring of Truth* (Vancouver, BC: Regent College Publishing, 2004).

2. Edythe Draper, *Draper's Book of Quotations for the*

Christian World (Carol Stream, IL: Tyndale House, 1992), 315.

3. Ibid., 316.

CHAPTER 3
The One Who Empowers

1. Pam Vredevelt, *Angel Behind the Rocking Chair* (Sisters, OR: Multnomah Books, 1997), 102.

2. Quote available online at http://www.worldnetdaily.com/news/printer-friendly.asp?ARTICLE_ID=48096 (accessed 8/22/06).

3. Quote available online at http://www.eonline.com/News/Items/0,1,18228,00.html (accessed 8/22/06).

4. Ibid.

5. Statistics available online at http://www.findarticles.com/p/articles/mi_qa3942/is_200007/ai_n8909440 (accessed 8/22/06).

6. Susan Mann and Ken Hulme, *A Second Chance: Daniel: Raised from the Dead. The 700 Club, CBN.com.*

7. Pam Vredevelt, *The Wounded Woman* (Sisters, OR: Multnomah Books, 2006), 62–64.

CHAPTER 4
The One Who Releases

1. Tim Rock, *Chuuk Lagoon Pohnpei and Kosrae* (Victoria, Australia: Lonely Planet Publications, 2000).

2. Cleon L. Rogers, *The New Linguistic and Exegetical Key to the Greek New Testament* (Grand Rapids, MI: Zondervan, 1998), 330.

CHAPTER 5
The One Who Transforms

1. Gary Richard, *View From the Zoo* (Nashville, TN: W Publishing Group, 1987), 68.

2. Gordon Fee, *God's Empowering Presence* (Peabody, MA: Hendrickson Publishers, 1994), 576, 579, 586.

3. Post-traumatic stress: Intense stress such as dangerous military conflict, rape, terrorist violence, involvement in a serious accident, kidnapping or natural disasters can leave difficult problems with anxiety. For years after the trauma, some have nightmares, irrational fears, depression, worry, and loss of interest in activities that once were pleasant. This persistent anxiety can occur in anyone following a traumatic experience.

4. Jack Hayford, *Hayford's Bible Handbook* (Nashville, TN: Thomas Nelson Publishers, 1995), 769.

5. Dr. Daniel Amen, *Change Your Brain, Change Your Life* (New York: Three Rivers Press, 1998), 9.

6. Michael Dy and Patricia Fancher, *The Genesis Process* (N.p.: Willford Graphics, 1998), 66.

7. S. Allsop, B. Saunders, M. Phillips, and A. Carr, "A Trial of Relapse Prevention With Severely Dependent Male Drinkers." *Addiction* 92, no. 1. (1997): 61–73.

8. Jack Hayford, Ed., *Spirit Filled Life Bible* (Nashville, TN: Thomas Nelson Publishers, 1991), 1967.

9. Charles Green, Notes from *Spirit Filled Bible* (Nashville, TN: Thomas Nelson Publishers, 1991), 760.

10. Cleon L. Rogers, *The New Linguistic and Exegetical Key to the Greek New Testament*, 542.

11. Quote available online at http://www.memorable-quotes .com/mark+twain,a99.html (accessed 8/22/06).

CHAPTER 6
The One Who Unites

1. John 16:7–11; *The Full Life Study Bible*, Zondervan, 1992; notes under Matthew 12:31, p. 1429. "For those who are worried about having committed the unpardonable sin, the very fact of wanting to be forgiven and the willingness to acknowledge wrongdoing is evidence that one has not committed the unpardonable sin."

2. Pam Vredevelt, *The Power of Letting Go* (Sisters, OR: Multnomah Publishers, 2006).

CHAPTER 7
The One Who Anoints

1. William A. VanGemeren, *New International Dictionary of Old Testament Theology and Exegesis* (Grand Rapids, MI: Zondervan, 1995), Vol. 3, 911.

2. James Moulton and George Milligan, *The Vocabulary of the Greek New Testament* (Grand Rapids, MI: Eerdmans, 1984), 693.

CHAPTER 8
The One Who Wars Through Us

1. Spiros Zodhiates, *The Hebrew Greek Study Bible* (Chattanooga, TN: AMG Publishers, 1996), 1643.

2. Jack Hayford, *Spirit Filled Life Bible*, 1848.

3. Spiros Zodhiates, *The Complete Word Study Dictionary New Testament* (Iowa Falls, IA: World Bible Publishers, 1992), 390–394.

4. Rick Renner, *Sparkling Gems from the Greek* (Tulsa, OK: Teach All Nations, 2003), 77.

5. Adrian Goldsworthy, *Roman Warfare* (London: Cassell

Wellington Hous, 2000), 125.

6. Rick Renner, *Sparkling Gems from the Greek*, 77.

7. Jack Hayford, *The Spirit Filled Life Bible*, NKJV, 1408.

8. Cleon L. Rogers, *The New Linguistic and Exegetical Key to the Greek New Testament*, 447.

9. C. Peter Wagner, *Acts of the Holy Spirit* (Ventura, CA: Regal Books, 2000), 75.

10. Sophie K. Scott, C. Catrin Blank, Stuart Rosen, and Richard J. S. Wise, *Brain*, Vol. 123, No. 12 (UK: Oxford University Press, December 2000), 2400–2406.

11. Ibid.

Additional Resources from
PAM VREDEVELT!

Are happiness and contentment far from your door? Resolve the negative emotions that weigh you down, and move boldly forward into the life of freedom God wants for you!

1-59052-598-1

1-57673-485-4

1-57673-636-9

1-57673-986-4

Exhaustion doesn't have to be habit-forming—overcome it with humorous and poignant vignettes that bring refreshment to the soul the way espresso brings energy to the body.

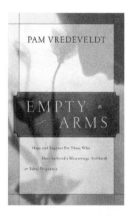

After the loss of her first baby, then bearing a fourth child with Down Syndrome, Pam Vredevelt now unveils with humor and touching insight her struggle to emerge into the light.

1-57673-644-X

Pam Vredevelt offers sound answers, advice, and reassurance to women experiencing the heartbreak of a miscarriage, stillbirth, or tubal pregnancy.

1-57673-851-5

The Wounded Woman is every woman's tool for releasing the hurts that hinder and moving forward to your glorious, liberated future.

1-59052-529-9

WWW.MULTNOMAH.NET/VREDEVELT

Multnomah® Publishers *Keeping Your Trust…One Book at a Time*®

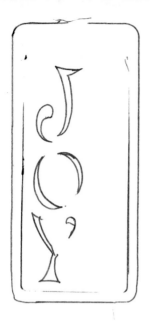